ON LINE

# ROMANIA
## in Pictures

Ann Kerns

Twenty-First Century Books

# Contents

Lerner Publishing Group realizes that current information and statistics quickly become out of date. To extend the usefulness of the Visual Geography Series, we developed www.vgsbooks.com, a website offering links to up-to-date information, as well as in-depth material, on a wide variety of subjects. All of the websites listed on www.vgsbooks.com have been carefully selected by researchers at Lerner Publishing Group. However, Lerner Publishing Group is not responsible for the accuracy or suitability of the material on any website other than www.lernerbooks.com. It is recommended that students using the Internet be supervised by a parent or teacher. Links on www.vgsbooks.com will be regularly reviewed and updated as needed.

Website address: www.lernerbooks.com

Twenty-First Century Books
A division of Lerner Publishing Group
241 First Avenue North
Minneapolis, MN 55401 U.S.A.

web enhanced @ www.vgsbooks.com

Library of Congress Cataloging-in-Publication Data

Kerns, Ann R.
    Romania in pictures / by Ann R. Kerns.
        p.   cm. — (Visual geography series)
    Rev. ed. of: Romania in pictures / prepared by Geography Dept., Lerner Publications Co., © 1993.
    Includes bibliographical references and index.
    ISBN-13: 978-0-8225-2497-7 (lib. bdg. : alk. paper)
    ISBN-10: 0-8225-2497-X (lib. bdg. : alk. paper)
      1. Romania—Juvenile literature.   2. Romania—Pictorial works—Juvenile literature.   I. Title.   II. Series:
Visual geography series (Minneapolis, Minn.)
DR206.K47 2007
949.8—dc22                                                                                    2005001429

Manufactured in the United States of America
1 2 3 4 5 6 - BP - 12 11 10 09 08 07

# INTRODUCTION

Romania is a nation of 22 million people in southeastern Europe. Romanians trace their origins to the Dacians, who occupied the region as early as 1000 B.C. Rome, an empire based on the Italian peninsula, conquered ancient Dacia at the beginning of the second century A.D. Roman colonists raised cities, built new roads, and introduced the Latin language to Dacia. After Rome withdrew from Dacia in the late third century, invaders from northern Europe and from Asia attacked eastern Europe. Further conflicts and invasions prevented Romanians from organizing independent states until the fourteenth century.

For much of their history, Romanians have lived in the shadow of stronger neighboring nations. In the fifteenth century, Hungarian landowners from central Europe and Turks from Asia Minor (modern Turkey) controlled large regions of Romania. Foreign political control slowed Romania's unification. Modern Romania came into being after World War I (1914–1918).

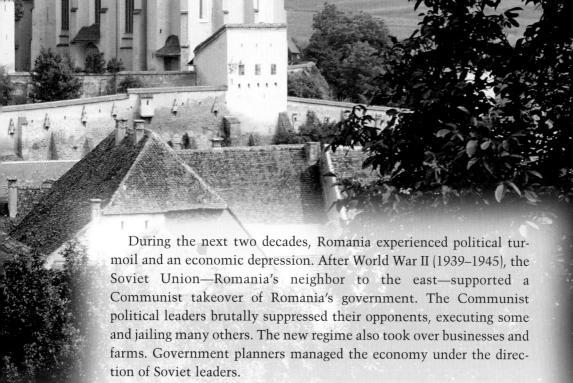

During the next two decades, Romania experienced political turmoil and an economic depression. After World War II (1939–1945), the Soviet Union—Romania's neighbor to the east—supported a Communist takeover of Romania's government. The Communist political leaders brutally suppressed their opponents, executing some and jailing many others. The new regime also took over businesses and farms. Government planners managed the economy under the direction of Soviet leaders.

Nicolae Ceausescu came to power in 1965. He was a Communist too, but he wanted to loosen Romania's ties to the Soviet Union. Under his leadership, Romania formed ties with non-Communist nations in Europe. Industrial production grew rapidly, but Ceausescu's government borrowed heavily to pay for new housing and factories. To repay these loans, the government cut back on imports (purchases from other countries) and increased exports (goods sold to other countries). This led to shortages of food and other necessities for

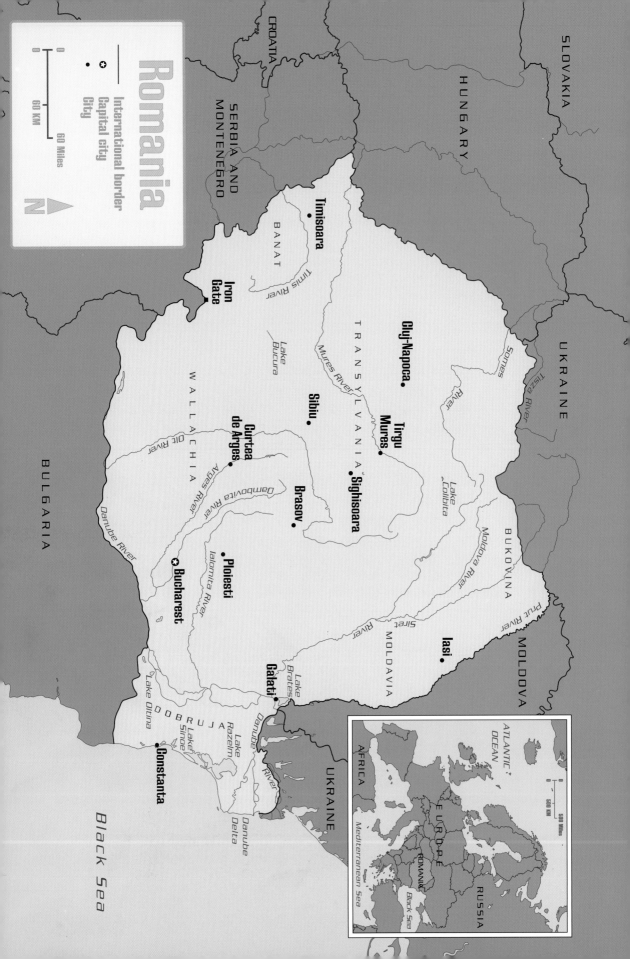

Romanians. By the late 1980s, a declining standard of living was causing serious hardship for most Romanians.

Ceausescu ruled as a dictator, a leader with absolute power. His government repressed political opposition, controlled the media, and restricted the lives of ordinary Romanians. In December 1989, the Romanian people rebelled against Ceausescu and overthrew his government. Soldiers arrested and executed Ceausescu and his wife, Elena.

Anti-Ceausescu leaders immediately took control of the government. A democratic election, the first in forty-four years, was held in May 1990. A 1991 constitution guaranteed civil rights. Romania's new president, Ion Iliescu, promised many changes. The government made strides toward a free market, an economy in which companies are privately owned rather than government-run.

But building a stable and democratic society has not come easily. Corruption (illegal practices) in government and in the court system still sparks mistrust among voters. Serious economic problems also hurt the country, which is one of the poorest in Europe. In parliamentary and presidential elections throughout the 1990s and the early 2000s, Romanians continued to demand steadier progress and faster reforms.

Romania hopes to join the European Union (EU) in 2007. The EU, an organization of European countries, will offer Romania greater economic and political ties to other European nations. To join, Romania must bring itself in line with EU standards on social issues (such as human rights and antidiscrimination laws) and economic practices (such as banking laws). Joining the EU is an important step forward for Romania in its long-term reform and development. Romanians also hope that their strong cultural heritage, rich natural resources, and an educated population will help the country overcome the legacy of Communist rule.

A quiet street in **Bistrita** showcases the architecture of fifteenth and sixteenth century merchants' homes in Romania. Bistrita was one of seven towns founded by the Saxons and dates to 1264.

# THE LAND

Romania is the largest nation in the Balkan Peninsula, a mountainous region in southeastern Europe. The peninsula lies between the Adriatic and Ionian seas on the west and the Aegean and Black seas on the east. In the north and east, Romania is bordered by Ukraine and Moldova. Other neighboring countries include Hungary to the northwest, Serbia and Montenegro to the southwest, and Bulgaria to the south. Between the Bulgarian border and a corner of Ukraine lies Romania's 130-mile (209-kilometer) Black Sea coast.

With a land area of 91,700 square miles (237,500 square km), Romania is slightly smaller than Oregon. The greatest distance from north to south is 320 miles (515 km). From west to east, Romania stretches 450 miles (720 km).

 ## Topography

Six historic names—Transylvania, Bukovina, Moldavia, Wallachia, Banat, and Dobruja—are used to describe Romania's regions. The landscape is almost equally divided among mountains, hills, and flatlands (plains and basins).

**MOUNTAINS AND HILLS** All Romania's mountain ranges belong to the Carpathian Mountain system. The Eastern, or Moldavian, Carpathians extend southward from the border with Ukraine. More than midway through the country, they curve west. This westward range is called the Southern Carpathians or Transylvanian Alps. The Western Carpathians include smaller ranges such as the Bihor and Banat mountains.

Several peaks in the Carpathians reach 8,000 feet (2,500 meters) in elevation. The Transylvanian Alps have the highest average elevation—5,000 feet (1,520 m). This range also includes the country's tallest peak, Mount Moldoveanu, at 8,343 feet (2,543 m). In the Carpathian's smaller ranges, the average elevation is 1,200 feet (360 m).

The Carpathians do not have the glaciers (slow-moving masses of ice) or large snowfields found in Western Europe's Alps. Instead, much

**The Carpathian Mountains** cover an area of 73,000 square miles (190,000 sq. km). It is Europe's second-largest mountain system. The Carpathians are separated from the largest European system, the Alps, by the Danube River.

of the Eastern Carpathians (from 1,500 to 6,000 feet, or 500 to 1,800 m) are covered in thick forests. The Bukovina region, at the northern end of the Eastern Carpathians, is very heavily forested.

The Transylvanian Alps have large grassy areas and some wooded regions. The alps also include more than 150 lakes carved out by prehistoric glaciers. The lowest of the ranges, the Western Carpathians, are the most densely populated.

Below the Carpathians to the south and east are the rolling hills of the Sub-Carpathians. The hills range in elevation from 1,300 to 3,300 feet (390 to 1,000 m). The Western Hills lie west of the Western Carpathians.

FLATLANDS The Carpathian Mountains form a circle around the Transylvanian Plateau, an elevated flatland. The plateau is the largest of Romania's flatland regions. Its plains, low hills, and river valleys make excellent farmland. To the east of Transylvania, Moldavia's hills and plains stretch down to the Prut River.

Plains also spread south and west. Between the Western Hills and the Serbia and Montenegro border, the Banat region is known for its farmland. And south of the Transylvanian hills, the Wallachian Plain rolls down to the Danube River.

In the southeast, the Dobruja region is a small plain between the northward stretch of the Danube River and the Black Sea. Dobruja has the country's lowest elevation. Some areas near the Black Sea are only a few feet above sea level. The region includes the Danube Delta, where the Danube River empties into the Black Sea. Most of the delta is

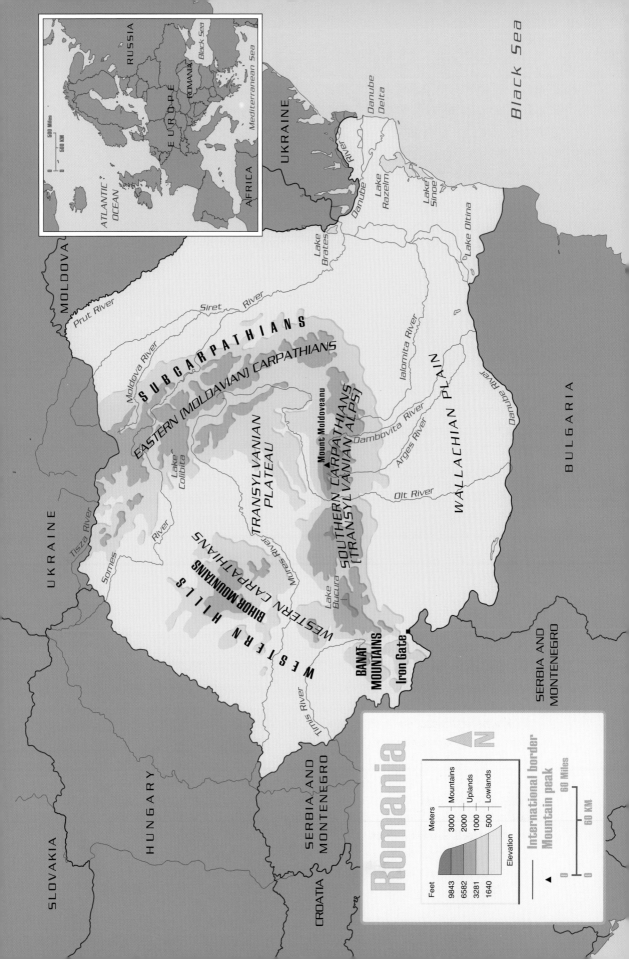

Black Sea

RUSSIA

Black Sea

EUROPE

Mediterranean Sea

ROMANIA

ATLANTIC OCEAN

AFRICA

500 Miles
500 KM

UKRAINE

Danube Delta

Danube River

MOLDOVA

Prut River

Lake Brates

Lake Razelm

Lake Sinoe

Lake Oltina

Siret River

Moldova River

SUBCARPATHIANS

EASTERN (MOLDAVIAN) CARPATHIANS

Ialomita River

WALLACHIAN PLAIN

Danube River

BULGARIA

Lake Colibita

TRANSYLVANIAN PLATEAU

SOUTHERN CARPATHIANS [TRANSYLVANIAN ALPS]

Mount Moldoveanu

Dambovita River

Arges River

Olt River

River

Tisza River

UKRAINE

WESTERN CARPATHIANS

Mures River

Somes

WESTERN HILLS

BIHOR MOUNTAINS

Lake Bucura

BANAT MOUNTAINS

Iron Gate

SERBIA AND MONTENEGRO

SLOVAKIA

HUNGARY

Timis River

SERBIA AND MONTENEGRO

CROATIA

Romania

N

| Meters | Feet |
|--------|------|
| 3000 Mountains | 9843 |
| 2000 Uplands | 6582 |
| 1000 Lowlands | 3281 |
| 500 | 1640 |

Elevation

International border
▲ Mountain peak

60 Miles
60 KM

## DANUBE DELTA

The Danube Delta has eighteen nature reserves. In these protected areas, hunting, fishing, tourism, lumbering, and development are not allowed. These areas allow native plants and trees to thrive. The protective restrictions also encourage birds and other wildlife to build habitats and breed.

More than 12,000 people also make their homes in the Danube Delta. Many live in reed cottages—small houses with stone walls and roofs woven from reeds. Most delta inhabitants make their living by fishing. Families also keep vegetable gardens, fruit trees, poultry, pigs, and honeybees.

wetlands—swamps, reed marshes, small lakes, and forests that flood in the spring and autumn.

## ◎ Rivers and Lakes

The Danube, at 1,865 miles (3,000 km), is one of Europe's longest waterways. It forms part of Romania's borders with Serbia and Montenegro and Bulgaria. The river crosses the Carpathian Mountains within a narrow pass known since ancient times as the Iron Gate. After flowing along the southern Romanian border, the Danube curves northward in Dobruja. There it branches into three parts before emptying into the Black Sea.

The Danube is Romania's most important river. The busy river carries passenger and commercial traffic from the Iron Gate to the Black Sea port of Constanta. It provides water for farming. And since the 1970s, when a hydroelectric power station was built at the Iron Gate, the Danube has been key to Romania's energy supplies. But the Danube has also suffered heavy pollution.

All of Romania's other major waterways are tributaries of (rivers that feed into) the Danube. The Mures River runs westward between the Transylvanian Alps and the Bihor Mountains before crossing Romania's border with Hungary. Other rivers flow southward from the Transylvanian Alps through Wallachia to the Danube. The Olt River has carved out a wide valley in the mountains before reaching the Wallachian Plain. The Arges and the Ialomita rivers cross eastern Wallachia near Bucharest, Romania's capital. The Dambovita River flows through Bucharest.

The Moldova and Siret rivers, which begin in the Carpathian Mountains, are the major waterways in Moldavia. The Prut River, which forms Romania's border with Moldova, meets the Danube just west of the Danube Delta.

Many of Romania's lakes were formed by prehistoric glaciers. The slow-moving ice dug out earth and rock to form lake beds. The

The Danube River narrows between the Iron Gate, a pass between the Carpathian and Balkan mountains in Serbia and Montenegro. The pass forms a natural border between the countries.

Transylvanian Alps have more than 150 small glacial lakes. These freshwater lakes are fed by mountain streams, rain, and snow. Other lakes in Romania lie near the Danube and other rivers. Some of Romania's lakes include Lake Colibita in northern Transylvania, the large glacial Lake Bucura, Lake Oltina on the Danube in Dobruja, and Lake Brates in eastern Romania.

Romania's largest lakes are saltwater lagoons along the coast of the Black Sea. These shallow bodies of water form along seacoasts. Two of Romania's largest lagoons are Lake Razelm (164 sq. miles, or 425 sq. km) and Lake Sinoe (66 sq. miles, or 171 sq. km).

## ⊙ Climate

Romania has a variable climate with warm summers and cold winters. Temperatures are generally lower in Romania's mountainous regions and higher in the plains of Moldavia and Wallachia.

The lowlands and plains of eastern and southern Romania experience greater temperature extremes. Bucharest averages 73°F (23°C) in July, the warmest month, and 27°F (–3°C) in January, the coldest month.

Precipitation is heaviest in Transylvania and in the Carpathian Mountains. In those regions, an average of 40 inches (102 centimeters) of rain and snow fall each year. On the plains, the average yearly precipitation is 20 inches (51 cm). Dobruja is Romania's warmest and driest region, with less than 15 inches (38 cm) of annual rainfall. But Dobruja's Danube Delta is the country's most humid area.

## ⊙ Flora and Fauna

Thick forests once grew on the plains and mountains of Romania. Romanians have cleared much of the land for settlement and for agriculture. But forests still cover about 30 percent of the country. Coniferous (evergreen) trees, such as pine and spruce, flourish in the Carpathians and in the higher elevations of Transylvania. Above the timberline—where temperatures are too low to support trees—hardy lichens and mosses take root in thin soil and on the surfaces of bare rocks.

Large, mixed forests of coniferous and deciduous (leaf-shedding) trees thrive in Transylvania. Deciduous trees, including birch, beech, and oak, favor the warmer climate of the plains. Willows and poplars line the banks of the Danube and other rivers. Reeds and more than one thousand other types of plants flourish in the swampy Danube Delta.

The growth of Romanian cities and farms has eliminated many natural wildlife habitats (homes for animals). But a wide variety of wildlife survives. Wild boars, bears, foxes, and chamois—small, goat-like antelopes—live in the Carpathians. Deer, wolves, and lynx also inhabit these mountains. Owls, woodpeckers, and jays inhabit the Carpathian forests. On the plains, polecats (animals related to weasels), rabbits, squirrels, and badgers are common.

The Danube Delta supports more than three hundred varieties of birds. Birds migrating between Europe, Asia, and Africa pass over the region. Nightingales, egrets, spoonbills, cormorants, geese, eagles, and ospreys nest and lay their eggs in the delta's marshes and forests. Large flocks of pelicans inhabit the northern delta. Other delta wildlife includes European minks, muskrats, wild boar, and many species of fish.

Fish are plentiful elsewhere in Romania. Trout flourish in mountain lakes. Pike, carp, flounder, and salmon live in the rivers and along the Black Sea coast. Eggs from Black Sea sturgeon provide caviar, an important Romanian export.

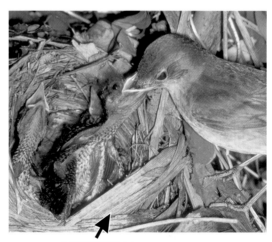

A female **nightingale** feeds her young. Nightingales are famous for their sad song. The **chamois** is a shy, swift animal prized for its skin, used to make a warm, soft leather.

# Natural Resources

Rapid growth of industry and cities during the twentieth century caused severe damage to Romania's natural environment. The government did not regulate pollution for many decades, and factories, mines, and waste fouled the air, water, and soil. The country's poor economic conditions made expensive environmental cleanup difficult. But in recent years, Romania has begun pollution control and cleanup to restore some of its natural resources.

Romania's most valuable mineral resources are natural gas and oil. Deposits of these fuels exist in the Carpathian Mountains and on the Transylvanian plateau. Dobruja and Moldavia also have coal deposits. Uranium, the fuel used in nuclear power plants, has been mined in Transylvania and Moldavia. But even with these resources, the country must import some natural gas, coal, and oil for heat and electricity.

Romania's minerals include iron ore, copper, zinc, and bauxite (the raw material used to manufacture aluminum). Gold and silver mines have been worked since ancient times in the northern Carpathians. Lead and salt deposits exist in Transylvania.

The current of the Danube River powers large hydroelectric plants. Reeds growing in the river's delta provide a fiber used to manufacture paper. Extensive forests in Transylvania and in the Carpathians supply lumber for Romania's building industry and for export.

A **hydroelectric dam** on the Danube River near Dragan harnesses water to provide electricity for parts of Romania. Hydroelectricity supplies about 29 percent of Romania's electricity production.

Romania's farmland is also a valuable natural resource. Forty-five percent of Romanians live in rural areas, and most make their living by farming. Farms produce food for the country and for export.

## Urban Centers

Romania is divided into forty-one *judete*, or counties. Each county is its own administrative district, or local government. Most of Romania's large cities are the seats of local governments.

BUCHAREST is Romania's national capital and largest city. It is the only city that is not part of a county. It is its own administrative district.

Bucharest's 2 million people represent 9 percent of the country's population. A commercial and transportation hub, Bucharest is also Romania's largest manufacturing center. It produces about 20 percent of the country's industrial output. Factories in the city produce machinery, aviation equipment, clothing, furniture, cosmetics, and electronic equipment. Several software and communications companies are also headquartered in Bucharest.

The city lies on the Dambovita River in eastern Wallachia. In ancient times, Bucharest grew as a settlement along a major Balkan trading route. In the eighteenth century, the city became the capital of Wallachia when that region was a state independent from Romania. In 1862, after Moldavia and Wallachia united to form Romania, Bucharest became the new nation's capital.

Foreign armies occupied the city during both World War I and World War II. Later, the Romanian Communist government destroyed historic buildings and entire neighborhoods to build modern office buildings, high-rise apartments, and a new presidential palace. A 1977 earthquake also destroyed many old buildings. But some historic districts and buildings survive, such as the Lipscani district and the Cotroceni Palace.

In the 1990s, Romania's population boom created a housing shortage in Bucharest. With a depressed economy, Bucharest could not afford to finish building projects or begin new ones. But after 2000, as Romania's economy grew, Bucharest's urban renewal began.

Visit www.vgsbooks.com for links to websites with additional information about the things to see and do in Romania's many cities, as well as links to websites about Romania's weather, natural resources, plants and animals, and more.

Ceausescu's government destroyed many historic buildings in Bucharest to make way for new construction. One of Ceausescu's projects was the massive **Palace of the Parliament,** a government building. At more than 3,767,000 square feet (350,000 sq. m), the palace is the largest building in Europe.

The city modernized its transportation systems and developed residential and commercial areas. The city's cultural life has also expanded with opera, theater, art galleries, and a wide variety of dance and music clubs.

IASI (pronounced yash) is a city of 350,000 in northeastern Romania. It is the capital of Iasi County and the historic capital of the region Moldavia. Located near Romania's border with Moldova, Iasi has been conquered and occupied several times. In the early nineteenth century, the city was a headquarters for the movement to unite the regions that make up modern Romania. Industries in Iasi include furniture and pharmaceutical factories, ironworks, and textile mills.

Iasi has many scientific and cultural institutes. The city is home to the Alexandru Ioan Cuza University of Iasi, the Natural History Museum, the National Theatre, the Science and Technical Museum, and many other literary and art museums.

CONSTANTA (population 340,000) is the capital of Constanta County. It is the largest port on Romania's Black Sea coast. Greek traders founded Constanta in the sixth century B.C. A canal links the port to the Danube River. From Constanta, Romanian companies import and export a wide variety of goods. Fishing and shipbuilding are other important industries. Tourists in Constanta enjoy Black Sea resorts, spas, and water sports. The extensive ruins of ancient Greek and Roman buildings and an annual wine festival also attract tourists.

**Cluj-Napoca** was founded in the 1100s by Germans. The city was known simply as Cluj until 1974, when then leader Nicolae Ceausescu joined Cluj with neighboring Napoca.

CLUJ-NAPOCA (pronounced kloozh NAH-po-kah), population 330,000, lies in northern Transylvania. For much of its history, Cluj-Napoca was controlled by Hungarians, and the city still contains a large Hungarian population. The city has one of the strongest economies in Romania. Factories in Cluj-Napoca produce chemicals, textiles, and ceramics. Babes-Bolyai University, with seventeen thousand students, has lent Cluj-Napoca a reputation as a young, stylish city. Coffeehouses, Internet cafes, and nightclubs are popular gathering places.

TIMISOARA (pronounced tih-mih-SHWA-ra) is the largest city in the Banat region, with a population of 320,000. Located on the Timis River, Timisoara is a commercial and industrial hub near the Serbia and Montenegro border. Factories in the city make chemicals, shoes, and electrical equipment. Timisoara has also become a cultural center, with theaters, libraries, and a major university.

Sometimes called the city of flowers, Timisoara features many parks, along with historic churches, fountains, and a central square, Piata Unirii.

BRASOV (population 320,000) lies on a high plateau in the foothills of the Transylvanian Alps. Founded by the Teutonic Knights (a German military group), Brasov dates to A.D. 1211. The capital of Brasov County, the city has become an important modern industrial hub with car and chemical factories. But Brasov has also preserved a central core of historic buildings. The town hall (built in 1420), the fifteenth-century Black Church, and the Poarta Schei (city gates) lend Brasov a medieval flavor.

Tourism is an important business in Brasov. It is easy to travel to and from Brasov and Bucharest, the Black Sea, and Transylvanian ski resorts. Many tourists also come to Brasov for an attraction that lies about 20 miles (32 km) out of town—Bran Castle. The castle is an imposing medieval fortress that once guarded Transylvania's frontier with Wallachia. A legend associates Bran Castle with Dracula, the fictional vampire. Although the legend is a mistake, it has made Bran Castle a popular sightseeing destination.

GALATI is the capital of Galati County, with a population of 300,000. Located on the Danube about 80 miles (130 km) from the Black Sea, the city has served as an international commercial port since the eighteenth century. Galati's port is used to import textiles and metals and to export timber and grain. The city also includes Romania's largest shipyard, its largest steel and iron plant, and several petroleum refineries.

Brasov's **Black Church** is the largest church between Istanbul, Turkey, and Vienna, Austria. Construction on the church lasted from 1383 to 1477. It was originally called Saint Mary's Church. But a 1689 fire coated the interior walls with soot, giving the church its current name.

# HISTORY AND GOVERNMENT

Humans and their prehistoric relatives have been living in the area of modern Romania for tens of thousands of years. Archaeologists have found tools and other evidence of settlement dating back to 100,000 B.C. But historians date Romanian heritage back to the Bronze Age, when humans developed bronze weapons and tools. The Bronze Age in Romania began during the 2000s B.C. During this time, nomadic (traveling) peoples from the north and west moved to the Carpathian Mountains and into the Danube River valley. They intermixed with the tribes already living in the area and created a farming culture. By the sixth century B.C., this culture was settled and distinct enough for Greek historians to refer to the people as the Thracians.

One Thracian group developed an independent state north of the Danube. This group prospered from trade with Greek merchants who had established ports along the western coast of the Black Sea. The group also controlled trade along the Danube. The Greeks called these people the Getae. The Romans later called the state Dacia and

its people the Dacii, or Dacians. The region's deposits of copper and iron ore enabled the Dacians to make strong weapons, and the Dacians gradually became one of the most powerful realms in southeastern Europe.

## ○ Roman Settlement

By the second century B.C., Rome was a growing empire based on the Italian peninsula. Roman soldiers were conquering large areas of the Balkan Peninsula. At first, the Romans and Dacians cooperated to build trading posts and fortifications in the Danube valley. But later, the Dacians fought the Romans for control of the region's resources. The Dacian king Burebista led violent raids on Roman settlements until his death in 44 B.C.

For years the Dacians both traded with Roman settlers and fought against the Roman army. In A.D. 88, the Romans dealt the Dacians a serious military defeat. The Roman emperor Domitian offered Dacian king Decebalus a peace agreement. In exchange for submitting to Roman rule, Decebalus was given money and military support.

Under this peace, Dacia thrived economically and grew larger and stronger. Within a few years, it grew strong enough to again present a threat to Rome. The Roman emperor Trajan was determined to conquer Dacia once and for all. In 101 Trajan's army crossed the Danube. After five years of battles, conquests, and rebellions, the Romans finally defeated the Dacians. In 106 Dacia became a Roman province.

Trajan posted a large Roman force in Dacia. He colonized the province with farmers, traders, and soldiers from other parts of the Roman Empire. The Romans built cities, roads, forts, mining operations, and farming estates. The colonists spoke Latin, the language of the Romans, and the Dacians eventually adopted this tongue. Modern Romania traces its name as well as its language to this period of Roman occupation.

## Migrations in Eastern Europe

Despite Rome's military strength, it could not adequately defend the province. Dacian rebels allied with Visigoths (Germanic tribes) and Sarmatians (nomads from the Near East) to besiege Dacian towns. The repeated attacks forced the Roman army to withdraw in 271. The Roman colonists and Dacian peasants remained behind, becoming the ancestors of modern Romanians.

From the third through the fifth centuries, Romania remained a violent and chaotic territory, with no organized government and weak defenses. Visigoths and other invading tribes such as the Huns, Bulgars, Slavs, and Avars destroyed homes and farms. Dacian and Roman inhabitants fled into the Carpathian Mountains and into Transylvania.

Meanwhile, the Roman Empire was weakening. It split into western and eastern halves. In the fifth century, the Western Empire collapsed after a series of invasions. The Eastern Roman (or Byzantine) Empire survived. Its capital was Constantinople (modern Istanbul, Turkey). The Byzantine Empire controlled lands south of the Danube.

From this region, Byzantine culture and religion spread northward through the Balkan Peninsula. Many Dacians and Romans adopted the Byzantine emperors' Christian faith. Later, when the Christian Church divided into Roman Catholic and Eastern Orthodox branches, Romania became an Orthodox stronghold.

## Magyars and Tatars Invade

In the late ninth century, central Asian Magyars—the ancestors of modern Hungarians—moved into southeastern Europe. The Magyars conquered lands along the Danube. They built new cities and converted to the Roman Catholic faith. Later, in search of fertile cropland,

**Stephen the Great** (975–1038) was devoutly religious and a patron of the arts. During his reign, he hired skilled architects to build new Orthodox churches and monasteries throughout Moldavia.

they pushed southward into Transylvania.

In the year 1000, the pope, the head of the Roman Catholic Church, crowned the Magyar leader Stephen I king of Hungary, a land that then included Transylvania. Stephen's successors tried to convert the people of Transylvania to Catholicism. But most Romanians in the region refused to abandon Orthodox Christianity.

To strengthen their control over Transylvania, Hungarian kings gave Transylvanian land to German Catholics from northern Europe. These German landowners adopted a political system called feudalism. Under feudalism, the landowners became the ruling class. Romanians remained the majority in Transylvania, but they were reduced to the status of peasants (owners of small farms) and serfs (landless workers on feudal estates).

By the thirteenth century, Hungary was losing its hold on Transylvania. Tatars from Asia swept across Moldavia and Transylvania and crushed Hungarian armies. But this only made life harder for Romanian peasants in Transylvania. Transylvania's ruling class demanded higher payments in crops from peasant farmers. They also began seizing land owned by peasants.

## ◉ New Principalities

To escape these harsh conditions, many Romanians fled Transylvania to settle lands east and south of the Carpathians. Some of these refugees established their own small states, known as *voivodates,* in Wallachia and Moldavia. Boyars—landowning nobles—in the voivodates raised money by renting their land to peasants.

Hungary attempted to control these regions, but the Romanians fought to keep their independence. During the fourteenth century, Romanians established principalities (regions ruled by princes) in Wallachia and Moldavia. Councils of boyars and Orthodox religious leaders elected the Moldavian and Wallachian princes. But frequent power struggles broke out among the boyars and the princes, weakening the principalities.

## Attack of the Ottoman Turks

In the fourteenth century, the Ottomans of Asia Minor attacked the Balkan Peninsula. The Ottomans, or Turks, first conquered lands south of the Danube. In 1396 they conquered Wallachia, then Moldavia.

The Turks, who practiced the Islamic religion, allowed Romanian princes to continue to rule their territories. But the princes were forced to pay tributes (money and goods) every year to the Ottoman sultan (ruler). In 1453 the Turks also captured the Byzantine capital, Constantinople, and overthrew the Byzantine Empire. Romanians had relied on Constantinople as a trading port, giving them access to the Black Sea. The city's conquest and the forced tributes caused economic decline in the Romanian principalities.

Resistance to the Turks continued after Constantinople fell. In the late fifteenth century, the Moldavian prince Stephen III (also called Stephen the Great) organized a military force of peasants. He tried to but could not convince other European rulers to join him in a crusade against the sultan. After Stephen's failed rebellion and death in 1504, the Moldavian nobles became vassals (feudal tenants) of the Turkish sultan.

## Michael the Brave

Encouraged by the weaknesses of the Romanian principalities, the armies of the sultan marched northward toward Hungary. The Turks scored a decisive victory at Mohacs in Hungary in 1526. Buda, the Hungarian capital, fell in 1541. After Hungary's defeat, the Turks allowed Hungarian nobles to rule Transylvania as a semi-independent region.

In Moldavia and Wallachia, the Ottoman sultan demanded ever-larger tributes. He appointed foreign princes as rulers. Most Romanians remained poor laborers. A few energetic and skillful leaders tried to improve conditions. Among them was Wallachian prince Michael the Brave. Michael led his forces into Transylvania in 1599 and allied himself with Hungarian nobles. The next year, he conquered Moldavia, bringing Wallachia, Moldavia, and Transylvania under a single Romanian leader for the first time.

Michael's success stirred his rivals to action. The ruler of the Habsburg Empire—a huge central European realm that controlled parts of Hungary—urged the Transylvanian nobles to resist Michael. In 1601 a Habsburg general arranged to have the Romanian leader assassinated. After Michael's death, Turkish control of the principalities resumed. Political turmoil and poverty worsened.

## Habsburg and Ottoman Rivalry

The Habsburg Empire also battled the Ottomans. In 1683 Habsburg armies repelled a Turkish siege of Vienna, Austria, the capital of the Habsburg Empire. In 1688 the Turks retreated from Transylvania, and by 1700 the region was brought into the Habsburg—or Austrian—Empire.

Other Romanian principalities tried to shake off Turkish rule. In 1711 Dimitrie Cantemir—a Moldavian leader—led a revolt against the Turks, winning the support of the Russian czar (emperor) and the prince of Wallachia. The uprising failed, but Cantemir's books and ideas awakened nationalism (a strong sense of ethnic identity) among Romanian-speaking people in the region.

After Cantemir's revolt, the Ottoman sultan appointed wealthy Greek aristocrats to rule Wallachia and Moldavia. These Greek rulers, the Phanariots, used the principalities solely to enrich themselves. The Phanariots heavily taxed the boyars and peasants in Moldavia and Wallachia. Many boyars lost their properties, and many peasants were reduced to serfdom.

In 1791 the Wallachian boyars asked the Russian czar for help in ending the rule of the Phanariots. This led to many years of conflict between Russia and Turkey over Romanian territory. In 1812 a treaty, the Peace of Bucharest, formally recognized Turkish control of Wallachia and the eastern part of Moldavia. Russia took over the western part of Moldavia, called Bessarabia (modern-day Moldova).

## A New Constitution

The Ottoman Empire began weakening in the nineteenth century. It was no longer able to control the vast territory it had conquered. Tudor Vladimirescu, a Wallachian army officer, saw this situation as an opportunity to overthrow Phanariot rule. In 1821 he led an uprising against the Phanariots. Vladimirescu died during the rebellion, but the Ottoman Empire agreed to begin appointing Romanian princes.

Russia invaded Moldavia and Wallachia in 1828, touching off another Russo-Turkish conflict. A treaty signed by Russia and Turkey in 1829 allowed Russian armies to occupy Moldavia and Wallachia. Although the principalities still belonged to the Ottoman Empire, Romanian princes were permitted to rule Moldavia and Wallachia for life.

In the 1830s, with Russian forces still in the region, Romanians drew up their first constitution, the Organic Statutes. The statutes called for an assembly of landowners to govern and for the unification of Moldavia and Wallachia. New laws also reformed the taxation and court systems, established public schools, and provided for an assembly to appoint future Romanian princes.

In Transylvania Hungarians pressed for the unification of the region with Hungary, then a part of the Habsburg Empire. Their opportunity came in 1848, as popular revolutions spread throughout Europe. Like many other Europeans, Hungarians demanded elected governments and an end to the privileges of monarchs (rulers such as kings and emperors) and nobles. In response to these demands, the Transylvanian legislature abolished serfdom and curbed the rights enjoyed by Transylvania's wealthy landowners.

The legislature also voted to join Transylvania with Hungary. The decision touched off a violent conflict in Transylvania between Hungarians and Romanians. Forces of the Austrian emperor—opposed to further Hungarian expansion—fought alongside the Romanians. After the Russian czar sent military forces into the region to help the Austrians, the fighting ended. Austria took control of Transylvania.

## Unification

The revolutions of 1848 inspired many Romanians to fight for a unified nation. New political parties pressed for complete independence from Russia and Turkey. After Russia lost a war against Turkey in 1856, a conference of several European powers guaranteed the political rights of Romanians in the principalities. Three years later, assemblies in Moldavia and Wallachia elected Colonel Alexandru Ioan Cuza as their prince. In 1861 the two principalities united to form Romania. The country's first national legislature began meeting in Bucharest.

Cuza passed important land reforms that ended serfdom in Moldavia and Wallachia and allowed freed serfs to own land. But corruption weakened his administration, and many Romanian legislators and landowners opposed the new laws. In 1866 army officers broke into Cuza's palace in Bucharest and forced him to resign his office. Prince Carol succeeded Cuza. Carol, a member of a European royal family, became the Romanian ruler through a plebiscite (popular vote).

Political conditions were also changing rapidly in Transylvania. In 1867 Austria was fighting wars on several fronts in central Europe. To compromise with the Hungarians, the Habsburg emperor Franz Joseph agreed to the creation of a dual (two-part) monarchy known as Austria-Hungary. Hungary then annexed (took over) Transylvania.

To learn more about Romania's many conquerors and other historical facts about the country, visit www.vgsbooks.com for links.

## Independence

In 1877 Russia and Turkey again went to war. The Romanians provided an army to help the Russians, who quickly gained the upper hand in the fighting. The Treaty of Berlin ended the conflict the next year. Russia and Turkey officially recognized Romanian independence and granted the northern part of the Dobruja region to Romania. (Bulgaria held southern Dobruja.)

In 1881 Romania's parliament proclaimed the nation a kingdom, and Prince Carol became King Carol I. Carol I sought to strengthen ties with western Europe. Romanian artists, writers, and politicians traveled to France to study, work, and exchange ideas. In addition, Carol's nephew and heir, Ferdinand, married Marie, the niece of Queen Victoria of Great Britain.

During Carol I's reign, new industries grew in several Romanian cities. Oil reserves discovered in Wallachia became a valuable export.

King Carol I (1839–1914)

The busy port of Constanta improved the nation's foreign trade. The government planned new roads and built rural schools. But even with these advances, many Romanian peasants and workers still suffered poor living conditions.

## Balkan Conflicts

By the beginning of the twentieth century, many Balkan countries had gained their independence from the Ottoman Empire. But conflict was still common in the region. Bulgaria and several of its allies fought and defeated Turkey in 1912. In 1913 Romania invaded Bulgaria and took control of southern Dobruja.

In the summer of 1914, the Balkan conflicts flared into an international war. The Central powers of Austria-Hungary and Germany fought against the Allied powers—Russia, Britain, and France. At the outbreak of World War I, the Romanian government hoped to stay out of the war. But in 1916, Romania joined the conflict on the Allied side.

That year Ferdinand—with promises of support from the Allies—sent forces into Transylvania to claim the region from Austria-Hungary. But Central power forces crushed the Romanian army. German forces marched into Bucharest, and the Romanian government fled the capital. Romania withdrew from the war.

In 1918, as the Central powers verged on defeat, Romania again fought for Transylvania. After the Allied victory in November, Romania gained Transylvania and part of the Banat region. Bessarabia declared its independence from Russia and joined Romania.

## Between the Wars

The Romanian legislature enacted sweeping changes in the postwar years. The legislature adopted a new constitution in 1923. The legislature attempted to meet poverty and political unrest in the countryside with a program of land reforms. The government also restructured and modernized Romania's industries.

In the early 1920s, a group of Romanian politicians formed the Romanian Communist Party. The Communists sought to put all property and industry under government control. A Communist government had already taken power in Russia (soon reorganized as the Soviet Union). But despite the powerful influence of Soviet Communism, the Romanian Communist Party remained very small for many years.

The Liberal Party was Romania's most powerful political organization during the 1920s. Ion Bratianu, a Liberal Party leader, became prime minister in the mid-1920s. The National Peasant Party, led by Iuliu Maniu, opposed the Liberal Party and gained the support of many rural workers. Maniu became prime minister after the National Peasant Party won elections in 1928.

In 1930 Ferdinand's son was crowned King Carol II. But Carol II's reign did not start well. The Great Depression (1929–1942) became a global economic crisis. Agricultural prices dropped severely, and unemployment spread through Romania. Politically, rivalry between the Liberal and National Peasant parties weakened the government, giving extreme political groups a chance to gain influence.

## The Iron Guard

One of those extreme groups was the Iron Guard. In the 1930s, the Iron Guard won support among Romanians unhappy with the country's divided parliament. The guard staged violent antigovernment demonstrations in Bucharest, and in 1933 guard members assassinated the Romanian prime minister, Ion Duca.

The Iron Guard was a Fascist group, relying on extreme nationalism and ethnic pride. It was also violently anti-Semitic, or prejudiced against Jews. Corneliu Codreanu, the Iron Guard leader, supported the German dictator Adolf Hitler. Hitler had come to power as head of the anti-Semitic Nazi Party in 1933.

Seeking to stop the growing unrest, Carol II assumed dictatorial powers. He suspended the Romanian legislature, abolished the constitution, and outlawed political parties. He ordered the arrest and execution of Codreanu and other leaders of the Iron Guard.

## World War II

As the political situation in Romania worsened, the rest of Europe braced for war with Hitler's Germany. In 1939 Germany invaded Poland and World War II began. Romania also worried about a German invasion. It sought the protection of France and Great Britain, leaders of the Allies. But by 1940, France and Great Britain were fighting their own battles against the Nazis. They could do little to help Romania.

Carol II agreed under pressure from Hitler to give up parcels of Romanian land, such as Bessarabia, to Bulgaria, to the Soviet Union, and to Hungary. Hitler also demanded access to Romania's valuable oil supplies. In September 1940, Ion Antonescu, a Romanian general allied with the Iron Guard and with Hitler, took control of the government. He forced Carol to resign. Carol's nineteen-year-old son, Michael, became the legal ruler of the country. But Antonescu controlled the army and the government.

Antonescu began persecuting and murdering Romanian Jews. His Iron Guards also began murdering political opponents. In October

A U.S. plane drops bombs on oil fields in Ploiesti during World War II.

1940, Antonescu allowed German forces to enter Romania, and in November Romania joined the Axis (the forces aligned with Germany). In June 1941, the Romanian army joined the Germans in an attack on the Soviet Union, an Allied power. Romanian forces pushed as far as southern Ukraine. But the Romanians and the Germans suffered a serious defeat at the Battle of Stalingrad in 1943.

By 1944 the tide had turned, and the Soviets were driving back the Axis forces. In Romania Antonescu came under attack from King Michael and from his political rivals. When Soviet troops arrived in the country, Michael and his allies overthrew Antonescu. Michael declared war on Germany and signed a peace treaty with the Soviet Union. A new government—made up of Romania's prewar parties as well as the Romanian Communist Party—took power.

By the spring of 1945, Germany had lost the war in Europe. The major Allied powers—the United States, the Soviet Union, Great Britain, and France—forged agreements on how to handle postwar arrangements. In both world wars, the Allies all had a common enemy that needed to be controlled—Germany. But soon after World War II, the alliance began to unravel.

> In theory, Communism eliminates many social problems by eliminating economic injustice. The government runs all companies and industries, and all workers share in the profits. But in practice, modern Communist governments often suppress any political opposition, censor the media, and control the private lives of citizens.

Soviet leader Joseph Stalin did not agree with democratic forms of government such as those used in the United States and many Western European countries. The Soviet Union was a Socialist republic. Its government was based on a form of Communism, a social and political system that developed in opposition to capitalism (the economic system used in the United States and Western Europe). Stalin's Soviet Union wanted to extend its political and economic control beyond its borders and into the Balkan Peninsula. It exerted its influence in many Eastern European countries by using local Communist parties.

## ◉ Postwar Development

In 1947, with the help of Soviet troops, Romania's Communist leaders took over the government. The Communists forced Michael to give up his throne. The country was renamed the People's Republic of Romania. The Communist Party drove all competing parties out of the government and had many opposition leaders arrested. Politicians, writers, and university professors were executed or jailed in concentration camps for criticizing the Communist regime. The government also began to nationalize (take over) banks, industries, and mines.

In 1948 Romania adopted a new constitution, putting the country under the leadership of a five-member state council. In 1952 Gheorghe Gheorghiu-Dej, the first secretary (leader) of the Romanian Communist Party, became the prime minister (the chief executive responsible for government policy).

Romania became a Soviet satellite, a country controlled by the Soviet Union. Under Soviet direction, new industrial companies were formed to control production of steel, oil, coal, and other important goods. These companies sent much of their output and half of their profits back to the Soviet Union. Romania's farms were collectivized—that is, private farmers were forced to combine their land into large operations called collectives. The government directed crop production, supplied farm equipment, and controlled the distribution of farm products (such as food).

Under industrialization, Romania enjoyed impressive economic growth in the 1950s and 1960s. The government built schools and installed electric power in many remote villages. But Soviet control of the economy prompted many Romanians—even Communists—to call for greater independence. In the mid-1960s, Romania forged closer trade and diplomatic ties with non-Communist nations in Western Europe.

## THE WARSAW PACT

World War II was followed by a period known as the Cold War (1945–1991). The Cold War pitted the United States and Western Europe against the Soviet Union. The war never broke out into actual battles. But Europe was effectively divided into East and West. Western European powers such as France and Great Britain have democratic rule and free-market economies. Eastern Europe, under the sway of the Soviet Union, adopted Communism. In 1949, most of Western Europe, the United States, and Canada formed the North Atlantic Treaty Organization (NATO), a military alliance. As more countries joined NATO in the 1950s, Communist countries came to view NATO as a threat and developed their own pact, or agreement. Eight Eastern European nations, including Romania, signed a treaty in Warsaw, Poland, in 1955. The Warsaw Pact was enforced by the Soviet Union, and the other pact countries became known as Soviet satellites. The Warsaw Pact and the Cold War lasted until 1991, when the Soviet Union collapsed.

In 1965 Nicolae Ceausescu became the head of Romania's Communist Party. He and two other Communist leaders ruled in a coalition until 1967, when Ceausescu became the president of the state council. At a party congress (meeting) in 1974, Ceausescu was elected Romania's president.

In the late 1960s, Ceausescu claimed increasing independence for Romania and called on Soviet leaders to withdraw their forces from Eastern Europe. As president, Ceausescu made several trips to the United States and signed an economic pact with the U.S. government. Romania also made agreements with European nations.

## 1989 Revolution

Within Romania, however, Ceausescu enforced a strict regime. Government bureaus censored (controlled the content of) all Romanian media, and the government jailed its opponents. Economic growth continued in the 1970s, but prices also rose. Romanians began to suffer shortages of food and consumer goods.

The Communist system of central planning and state ownership of the economy led to corruption and inefficiency. Many industries used outdated equipment, and the government did not invest in new machinery. In addition, Ceausescu used public funds for massive building projects in Bucharest. He and his family also used public money for lavish personal expenses.

To pay for its industrial growth, Romania borrowed heavily from Western European nations and from the United States. Determined to repay this debt, Ceausescu saved money by limiting imports of essential food, energy, and consumer goods. These policies and the falling production in Romanian factories further damaged the economy in the late 1980s.

Discontent with Ceausescu's Communist rule erupted into violence in the late 1980s. Many Romanians took to the streets to demonstrate against the injustices and poverty they suffered. In December 1989, in Timisoara, a large demonstration against Ceausescu ended in a massacre of citizens by government security forces. Street battles in Bucharest and Brasov killed hundreds of people. As riots continued in the capital, several of Ceausescu's own army units joined the anti-Communist demonstrators. When Ceausescu and his wife, Elena, attempted to flee, they were captured by soldiers. After a secret trial, the Ceausescus were executed on December 25.

Ceausescu's fall brought the National Salvation Front to power. The front was a political party led by former Communist officials. Ion Iliescu, the party's leader, became the Romanian president, the official head of state. Open elections in 1990 gave the front a majority in the legislature.

A memorial in Bucharest commemorates those killed in the 1989 revolution. The black circles on the wall mark bullet holes.

On December 8, 1991, voters approved Romania's new constitution. It promised freedom of the press, freedom to form political parties, and other democratic principles that give voters a voice in their government. But many Romanians suspected that Iliescu's government, made up of former Communists, would do little to ensure a democratic system. And in fact, the government made few political and economic reforms. Opposition parties, however, failed to unite behind a challenger, and Iliescu was reelected in 1992.

Throughout the early 1990s, reform was slowed by pro-government and antigovernment protests. Workers' rights groups such as labor unions also staged riots and strikes. Foreign governments were reluctant to invest in Romania while the political situation remained unstable. The economy failed to develop. In 1996 a candidate in favor of more radical reform, Emil Constantinescu, was elected president. His party, the Democratic Convention, also won a majority of seats in the legislature (lawmaking body). But economic progress remained slow through the 1990s.

## Recent Developments

Constantinescu, his party, and his political allies were elected on promises of reform. They promised to clean up political corruption—bribery, graft (illegal financial deals), control of the media, and other practices left over from the Soviet-style government. They also promised to improve the standard of living by moving toward a free-market economy (an economy based on free competition and private ownership of businesses). But by 2000, Romanian voters felt that the Constantinescu government had failed to make any real changes.

That year voters once again elected Iliescu president. As head of the president's party, the Social Democratic Party, Adrian Nastase became prime minister. Under Nastase, the Social Democratic Party formed a coalition, or political alliance, with the Democratic Union of Hungarians in Romania, a party of ethnic Hungarians.

The coalition stabilized Romania's government for the next four years. The country joined NATO. It also initiated political and social reforms that moved Romania closer to winning membership to the EU. In 2003 voters approved major amendments to the Romanian constitution, to bring Romanian law into compliance with EU standards. Romania hopes that the EU will provide support in economic development, foreign policy, human rights, and other areas.

After four years, however, Romanian voters decided that Iliescu and Nastase had not pushed hard enough for reforms. In December 2004, Traian Basescu, the popular mayor of Bucharest, beat Nastase in the presidential election. Basescu appointed Calin Tariceanu prime minister. Like post-1989 governments before them, Basescu and Tariceanu say they will focus on ending corruption, relieving poverty and other social problems, and preparing Romania for EU membership.

## ▶ Government

Romania's government is based on the country's 1991 constitution and on 2003 amendments. The constitution declares that Romania is a republic, in which voters elect officials to govern on their behalf. The government consists of executive, legislative, and judiciary branches.

The president is the official chief executive and the head of state. He or she is elected by a popular vote to a term of five years. The president may serve a maximum of two terms. The president nominates a prime minister, and the legislative branch must confirm the nomination. After confirmation, the prime minister selects a cabinet—a group of ministers who advise the president and prime minister. Cabinet members must also be confirmed by the legislature.

Romania's legislature is organized as a parliament. The parliament, called the National Assembly, has two chambers. The Chamber of Deputies has more than 300 members, and the Senate has about 150 members (exact numbers depend on the population). Voters aged eighteen and older elect National Assembly members to four-year terms.

Romania's judiciary consists of a system of courts of law. Local courts hear routine criminal and civil cases. County courts can hear more important criminal and civil cases and cases involving commercial law, such as bankruptcies. They can also hear appeals on decisions made in local courts. Courts of Appeal hear appeals on county court cases and can also hear very serious criminal and civil cases. The Supreme Court is the court of last resort for appeals—the last court in which a defendant can ask that a lower court decision be overruled.

Romania also has a Constitutional Court. The Constitutional Court makes sure that laws passed by parliament follow the principles of the constitution. The Constitutional Court consists of nine judges appointed by the president and the National Assembly. Other Romanian courts include a Court of Accounts (which make sure government funds are properly spent) and military courts.

On a local level, Romania's forty-one counties and the district of Bucharest have their own elected councils, which administer local government business. Cities and towns also have councils or mayors. The central, or national, government appoints prefects to oversee the actions of local authorities.

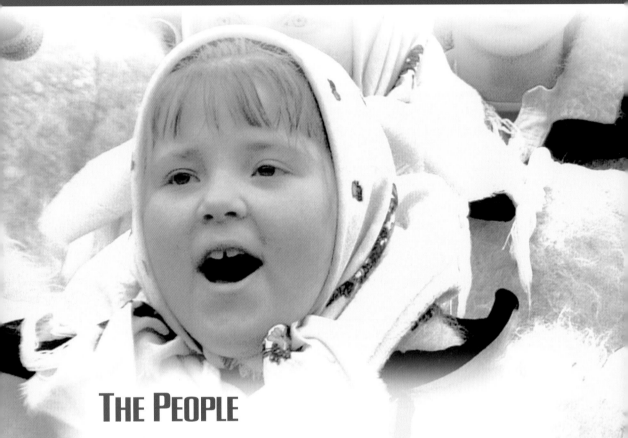

# THE PEOPLE

At the beginning of the twentieth century, most Romanians lived in the countryside. Wealthy landowners, family farmers, and peasants all depended on agriculture for their incomes. But after World War II, Romania became more industrialized. Industrialization is economic development based on manufacturing. Most of the factories that sprang up with industrialization were built in cities and towns. People began moving to urban centers for jobs, and the cities and towns grew. In many ways, modern Romania remains split between rural and urban cultures.

Almost half of modern-day Romanians live in rural areas. Romania's most intensive agriculture is located on the plains, and they have the largest rural populations. Higher elevations are the most sparsely populated areas. Many rural Romanians live in small wooden cottages. They decorate their homes with traditional arts and crafts, and they celebrate holidays and special occasions in traditional ways.

Urban centers are densely populated, with many people living in crowded apartment buildings. Like rural Romanians, urban dwellers

enjoy traditional culture. But they are also exposed to more international influences in venues such as museums, movie theaters, and
music clubs.

## Ethnic Groups

About 89 percent of the country's 22 million people are ethnic
Romanians. They are descended from Romania's ancient settlers—the
Dacians, Romans, and tribes such as the Goths and Slavs. Modern
Romania has only a small influx of immigrants from other countries,
but it is home to several groups of historical ethnic minorities.

About 7 percent of Romanian citizens claim Hungarian ancestry.
Most of the country's Hungarians live in the regions of Banat and
Transylvania. Hungarians make up a majority in the region surround-
ing the city of Tirgu-Mures, near the geographic center of Romania.

The Roma people are the second-largest ethnic group in Romania.
Exact numbers for the Roma population are unclear. Some Roma are

# THE ROMA MINORITY

The Roma people, or Romani, were once called Gypsies, because of an old belief that the Roma came from Egypt. Modern historians have determined that the Roma were brought to Romania as slaves of the Ottoman Turks.

Traditionally, the Roma do not take part in routine life in Romania. Some Roma are nomadic, but even when settled, the Roma live in communities separate from the larger population. Many are unemployed or do odd jobs. Many Roma children do not go to school regularly. Most Roma remain without a formal education.

Critics claim the Roma way of life has made the minority a nuisance. Roma often beg on city streets, in front of shops and restaurants. Many Romanians view the Roma as frightening or, worse, criminal. Police statistics suggest Roma commit a majority of thefts and other crimes in Romania. But Roma defenders claim that the minority is forced into begging and crime because they face serious poverty and discrimination. Romanian employers, defenders say, will not hire Roma, and the government shows little support for educational or social programs targeting the minority.

A **Romani couple** and their dog sit in their makeshift residence—a small lean-to tent.

nomadic (without a fixed residence), so they are often not counted in censuses. Other Roma identify themselves on censuses as Romanian or Hungarian. Official estimates put the Roma population at about 2.5 percent. But some social welfare groups suggest that as many as 2 million Roma live in Romania, making them almost 10 percent of the population.

Ethnic Germans are Romania's third-largest minority. They are the descendants of German farmers who came to Romania from the twelfth through the eighteenth century. However, the number of ethnic Germans in Romania has declined steeply. Many have chosen to move to Germany for better jobs.

Other minorities in Romania include Ukrainians, Serbs, Croats,

Russians, Turks, and Tatars (descendants of Ottoman Turks). These minorities together account for about 1.5 percent of the population.

## Daily Life

Romania has not adjusted to post-Communist life as well as some other Eastern European countries have. Its economy has grown stronger since 2000, and several industries—from agriculture to information technology—provide a variety of jobs. But these factors have not yet translated into better wages for average Romanians.

Romanians remain among the poorest people in Europe. Almost one-third of Romanians live below the poverty line. For those people, their incomes do not cover their most basic expenses, such as food and shelter. In late 2005, the average monthly wage, before taxes, was 965 lei (about U.S. $313). In contrast, the average monthly wage in neighboring Hungary was equal to U.S. $748.

Even many Romanians living above the poverty line have little money for luxury items. Cars, color televisions, and personal computers are becoming more common, but they are still out of reach for many. But for a country plagued by poverty and political problems left over from previous eras, Romania has a vibrant culture. Romanians enjoy traditional and modern music and literature. They have a strong tradition of hospitality, and many gatherings center on sharing food with family and friends. Romanians also display a commitment to education, and many—especially young people—speak more than one foreign language.

**Traditional dress** is a common sight in the Maramures region of Romania. For links to more information about Romania's strong cultural traditions, visit www.vgsbooks.com.

## Education

According to Romanian law, children between the ages of seven and fourteen must attend elementary school. After that, students can decide to continue to secondary school. Most Romanian students attend secondary school for at least two years. Education and literacy (the ability to read and write) are considered key to Romania's future as a modern European country. The country's literacy rate is 98 percent.

Romania has five types of secondary schools. Government testing determines which type of school best suits each student. General education schools prepare students for university. Art and music schools and physical education schools provide general education courses while allowing students to concentrate on special studies. Teacher training schools prepare students for careers in education. And vocational schools prepare students for jobs in electrical work, auto repair, and other similar industries.

During Ceausescu's rule, Romania's entire educational system was strictly controlled by the government. Students were taught Communist political theory. Ceausescu also stressed the importance of nationalism. In primary and secondary schools, classes focused on practical studies and rote learning (memorizing information). In universities, scholars did not exchange research or information with

Students in Romania must attend **elementary school** for seven years.

**The National Library** in Bucharest was founded in 1836.

scholars from other countries. After the 1989 revolution, many educational reforms began. Teacher training and standards for curricula (subjects taught) improved. Schools were repaired, and classrooms were furnished with more modern equipment and supplies. But the reforms are ambitious and have not yet been completed.

The country's oldest higher education institution is the University of Bucharest, founded in 1864. Cluj-Napoca and Iasi also have large, long-established universities. Since 1989 many more universities and technical institutes have been established in other cities, such as Timisoara and Constanta. The National Library and the Romanian Academy in Bucharest are also important to university study and research. The library and academy each house millions of books and periodicals.

## Health Care

Under the Communist government, health care in Romania was free. The government trained and hired doctors and nurses and built hospitals throughout the country. This raised the life expectancy rate—the average age at which people die. It also lowered the infant mortality rate, which measures the number of children who die in the first year of life. But in the 1980s, under Ceausescu, support for health care lapsed. Death rates climbed, and more children were stillborn or died in early infancy. Poor hospital practices for babies, such as not properly testing blood used in transfusions and reusing vaccination needles, led to an increase in deadly diseases such as

## STREET CHILDREN

Under Ceausescu's rule, tens of thousands of Romanian children ended up in orphanages. Romania has worked to improve that situation. The government closed many large orphanages and tried to place abandoned children in foster care or back with family members. In 2001 Romania also banned international adoptions in an effort to end child trafficking, or the illegal selling of abandoned children. But these measures added to another crisis. About two thousand children in Romania live on the streets, mostly in large cities such as Bucharest.

Charity workers say that many street children are victims of failed foster care. Others were not wanted by the biological families they were returned to. Rather than face abuse or neglect at home, the children run away. On the streets, they join informal "families" of other street children. But many are sexually or physically abused by older children or by adults. The children have to beg or steal for food. Many turn to substance abuse, such as drinking alcohol or sniffing glue. International and Romanian charity workers try to help the street children. But the number of homeless children has not decreased.

pediatric AIDS (acquired immuno-deficiency syndrome).

To counter the high death rates, Ceausescu tried to encourage people to have babies. He enacted strict laws against birth control and abortion. But most Romanians could not afford to feed and clothe large families. And if a child had a medical condition or special needs, the family could often not afford the necessary treatment. Poor families began placing sick or unwanted children, including those with AIDS, in orphanages. These institutions were often dirty and understaffed. The children were not properly cared for and had little hope of being adopted. After Ceausescu's death, Western charity workers were shocked to discover how large the Romanian orphanage system was and how bad conditions were.

Since the 1989 revolution, health care has improved. The government increased spending on the health-care system, including raising the salaries of doctors and nurses. The health-care system was also decentralized—control over the operations of clinics and hospitals shifted from the central government to local administrators. Local administrators can address problems and community health needs directly.

But poverty still takes its toll. Romania's infant mortality rate—about 27 deaths per 1,000 live births—is one of the highest in Europe. Many infant deaths are caused by food shortages, poor care for expectant mothers, or inadequate medical facilities. Romania's average life expectancy is also low by European standards. At 71 years, it falls far behind countries such as France (79 years) and Germany (78 years). Cancer, heart disease, and alcoholism are the most serious health problems among adults.

Romania has done well in the fight against AIDS. A 2004 estimate suggested that only about 10,000 Romanians were infected with HIV (the virus that causes AIDS) or had the full-blown disease. In comparison, nearby Ukraine has about 300,000 AIDS cases. But more than 70 percent of Romania's AIDS patients are young—teenagers who were infected as babies in the late 1980s and early 1990s. Romanian's post-Communist government at first struggled to find money to buy expensive AIDS drugs. But since 1997, the national AIDS budget has risen from $3 million to $30 million. Unprotected sex and heroin use (which spreads the disease through shared hypodermic needles) still add to the number of infected adults. But Romania's success in treating AIDS babies and controlling the disease has outshone many wealthier countries' efforts.

Want to learn more about daily life and education in Romania? Visit www.vgsbooks.com. There you'll also find links to more information about Romania's diverse ethnic groups.

# CULTURAL LIFE

Romanians are proud of their cultural heritage. They have a unique language, a long tradition of literature and art, and a love of music. Romanian culture is a blend of folk traditions, European influences, and modern trends.

## ◗ Language

Like French and other Romance languages, Romanian is based on Latin, the language of ancient Roma. Its Latin origin makes Romanian very different from the languages used in neighboring countries. Over the centuries, however, Greek, Slavic, and Turkish words have been introduced into the Romanian vocabulary.

Romanian is the official language and is spoken throughout the country. But ethnic minorities, such as Germans and Hungarians in Transylvania and Banat, also speak their own languages. The Ceausescu government banned non-Romanian media. But Hungarian and German newspapers and television programs

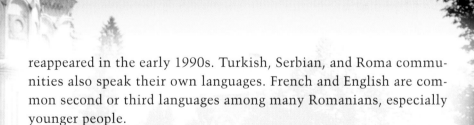

reappeared in the early 1990s. Turkish, Serbian, and Roma communities also speak their own languages. French and English are common second or third languages among many Romanians, especially younger people.

## Religion

Romania's Communist leaders passed many laws to restrict religious worship. Communist theory views religion as backward and superstitious. And for many Communist governments, the influence of religion and clergy is a threat to a government-controlled society. In Romania the Communists seized church land and closed or destroyed some churches. Many of the destroyed churches were hundreds of years old and filled with priceless artwork. Communist Party authorities followed and harassed churchgoers and arrested priests and ministers who spoke out against Communism. Government-controlled media sharply criticized religious faith and practices. Despite these restrictions, many Romanians kept their beliefs. And after the 1989 revolution, the government began restoring Romanians' freedom of religion.

The Romanian Orthodox Church, a Christian denomination, remains the largest religious institution in Romania. About 87 percent of the population belongs to the Orthodox Church. The church is a branch of the Eastern Orthodox Church, which also includes the Greek Orthodox and the Russian Orthodox churches.

Many Hungarians and Germans living in Romania belong to the Roman Catholic Church. Another important branch of Catholicism in Romania is the Uniate, or Eastern Rite, Church. Uniate members accept the authority of the pope in Rome but practice Orthodox religious rites. Catholics represent about 6 percent of the population. Another 6 percent of Romanians belong to Protestant Christian denominations, such as the Lutheran Church.

Romania's Jewish population has steadily declined since World War II. Before the war, 800,000 Jews lived in Romania. During the war, Jews suffered persecution by both the Romanian government and the German army. As in Nazi Germany, many Jews were sent to prison camps, where they died. Others were murdered in pogroms, or organized assaults on communities. The war reduced the Jewish population to 450,000. And after the war, many Jews emigrated from Romania to Israel, a newly formed Jewish state in the Middle East. In modern Romania, there are fewer than 10,000 Jews, mostly in Bucharest and in Moldavia. Other religious minorities in Romania include Muslims (mostly Tatars and Turks living in the Dobruja region) and Greek Orthodox.

## ELIE WIESEL

Elie Wiesel was born in 1928 in a small Jewish community in Sighet, Transylvania. When World War II began, the Wiesel family believed they were safe from the violence endured by Jews in Germany and Poland. But in 1944, Nazi soldiers arrived in Sighet. Fifteen-year-old Elie, his family, and Sighet's other Jews were rounded up and sent to Nazi concentration camps. The Wiesels were sent to the infamous camp in Auschwitz, Poland. Wiesel's parents and a sister died at Auschwitz, but he survived. After the war, he moved to France and recorded his memories of Auschwitz in his book *Night*. He later moved to New York City, wrote many other books and articles, and became a human rights campaigner. In 1985 Wiesel was awarded the U.S. Congressional Medal of Honor, and in 1986 he was awarded the Nobel Peace Prize.

Visit www.vgsbooks.com for links to websites with additional information about religion in Romania, including the country's many historical monasteries.

## Literature

The earliest Romanian literary works were ballads—poetry set to music and sung aloud from memory. Orthodox church leaders wrote the first Romanian religious texts in the fifteenth century. These texts were written in Cyrillic, the alphabet used in Russian and Slavic languages. In the eighteenth century, historical writing became the most popular form of literature. Romanian historians, including Dimitrie Cantemir, proudly traced the story of their nation back to the settlement of the country by the Romans.

Beginning in the nineteenth century, Romanian authors drew on native Romanian folk stories for inspiration. In the 1860s, Romanian writers stopped using the Cyrillic alphabet. Instead, they began using the Roman alphabet (used in French, English, and other Western languages). This event symbolized Romania's cultural connection to western Europe, and this period is seen as the start of modern Romanian literature. Romanian authors wrote plays, poetry, and novels about politics, culture, society, and folk traditions.

In 1863 Titu Maiorescu and other writers established the Junimea Society. The society's literary journal, *Convorbiri literare* (literary discussions), published some of the period's great writers. These writers included Mihai Eminescu, a poet from Moldavia, and Ion Luca Caragiale, a playwright from Wallachia.

In the twentieth century, Romanians contributed to new modern styles of literature. The Romanian writer Tristan Tzara, who settled in France after World War I, took part in the Dadaist movement, which attacked conventional art forms. Lucian Blaga was an expressionist poet, basing his work on intense emotion. Perhaps the Romanian writer to gain the most international fame was Eugene Ionesco. Like Tzara, Ionesco spent much of his life in France, where he became a famous playwright in the 1950s. His works are part of the Theatre of the Absurd movement. His plays such as *The Lesson* and *Rhinoceros* describe the absurdities and loneliness of modern life.

During Communist rule, most published writing reflected the government's political influence. Writers who disagreed with Communism often left Romania to work in France and other countries. The Ceausescu regime was especially difficult for writers. Dissidents (those who disagree with the government) were harassed and even arrested.

In post-Communist Romania, writers have struggled with political conflict and social change. In the 1990s and 2000s, some writers also see a struggle in the global market. They want to express their unique Romanian heritage but must also compete for readers against mass media and popular culture—pop music, Hollywood movies, and foreign books and magazines. Contemporary Romanian writers include Tudor Arghezi, Mihai Beniuc, Marin Preda, Veronica Porumbacu, and Maria Banusi.

## Art

Romanian painting dates back to ancient times, when Dacian potters decorated their wares with elaborate geometric designs. Beginning in the fourteenth century, the painting and architecture of the Byzantine Empire influenced artists and builders in Wallachia and Moldavia. Byzantine art is known for its rich colors, gold backgrounds and trim, and domed buildings. The monastery in Curtea de Arges in Wallachia strongly reflects Byzantine style.

Romania is also famous for churches and monasteries decorated with frescoes (paintings done on wet plaster). During the first part of the fifteenth century, Stephen the Great ordered forty-eight churches built in Moldavia to celebrate his victory over the Turks. Those churches were lightly trimmed with fresco painting. But beginning in the sixteenth century, artists in Bukovina in northeast Romania took fresco painting to new heights. The artists covered monasteries and churches, inside and out, with frescoes depicting biblical and

**Sucevita Monastery** in Bukovina is the largest and last of the painted monasteries to be built. The monastery was built between 1582 and 1601, with the exterior frescoes dating from about 1590.

This icon appears in a monastery in Neamt, Romania.

## ICONS

Icons, or religious paintings, are very important in the Orthodox faith. Saints or sacred events are depicted in traditional styles on the hand-painted wooden or glass icons. In churches, large icons hang on the walls lit by candles or oil lamps. In Orthodox homes, families often pray together in front of their icons. Icons are also carried during Easter processions, weddings, and other religious ceremonies.

historical scenes. The paintings told visual stories to peasants who could not read. Many of Bukovina's painted churches and monasteries survive. Some of the most well-preserved examples are in Humor, Moldovita, Sucevita, and Voronet.

Painting in Romania reached an artistic peak during the nineteenth century, when many Romanian artists studied at academies in western Europe. The painter Theodor Aman, a famous portraitist, worked in a traditional style. Nicolae Grigorescu illustrated rural people in the natural settings of his landscape paintings.

After World War II, Socialist realism required artists to render industrial workers and Communist leaders in flattering or heroic poses. The government forced all the country's artists to join a tightly controlled union and forbade the use of abstract shapes and symbols in painting and sculpture.

The most famous Romanian artist of the postwar period escaped these restrictions by leaving the country. Constantin Brancusi was an abstract sculptor who lived in France. Brancusi molded wood and

**The Merry Cemetery** in Sapanta features wooden cross headstones painted blue, traditional colors of hope and freedom. Folk art pictures and witty words inscribed into each cross tell the life story of the person buried underneath each one.

bright metal into long shapes and geometric forms to idealize people and nature. Museums and private collectors around the world have purchased Brancusi's elegant sculptures.

Romania also has a strong tradition of folk art and handicrafts. Weavers still produce rugs by knotting natural wool yarn on wooden looms. Furniture from different regions of the country carries elaborate designs in a variety of materials. Traditional linen, embroidered clothing, and handmade lace are still common in many rural homes in Romania. Painting religious icons, egg decorating, and basket weaving are also traditional Romanian crafts.

## ◉ Music

Music is a favorite pastime in Romania. Cities often host symphony orchestras, soloists, and choirs. Residents and visitors enjoy folk and jazz festivals held in Bucharest and other cities. Throughout Romania, many professional and amateur groups perform folk songs known as *doinas* and the national dance, the hora.

Romania's best-known classical musician is Georges Enesco, a violinist who wrote a famous series of rhapsodies (musical pieces) based on Romanian folk melodies. Bucharest holds a festival of Enesco's music every three years. The Romanian pianist Dinu Lipatti gained international recognition as a performer and orchestral conductor. And more recently, soprano singer Angela Gheorghiu has become an international opera star.

Popular music gained momentum in Romania in the 1940s and 1950s, with romantic songs and dance music. Gheorghe Zamfir (born in 1941) became known internationally during the 1960s.

**The hora** is a popular Romanian folk dance in which the dancers form a big circle. Romanians dance the hora at weddings, festivals, and rural gatherings.

Zamfir played romantic, emotional music on an instrument called the panflute.

Rock music also became popular in the 1960s as Romanians imported Western acts such as the Beatles and the Rolling Stones. But pop and rock musicians, like artists and writers, had to censor themselves to avoid problems with government officials. Ceausescu, in particular, tried to repress any outside influences on his idea of a national Romanian culture. One longtime band, Phoenix, survived by combining rock with traditional Romanian music. Phoenix formed in 1962 and released its latest album in 2005.

Western European and American music continue to influence Romanian performers. Hip-hop, rap, and dance music are all very popular. But Romanian performers still often incorporate traditional music and write lyrics about Romanian life and politics. Some popular acts include Hi-Q (a trio who often appear on TV), B.U.G. Mafia (a rap group), Luna Amara (a rock group), and Nicoleta Alexandru (a pop singer).

## Food

Romanian cuisine has a rich tradition that borrows from Turkish and Greek cooking. A favorable climate and fertile soil contribute to the wide variety of vegetables and grains used in Romanian dishes. Romanians also enjoy meat, especially pork and beef.

Many Romanians eat a light breakfast and enjoy their main meal in the early afternoon. For a first course, cooks prepare soups with meat, vegetables, or noodles. *Borsh* is a thick cabbage soup traditionally made with bran. *Ciorba* are soups cooked with lamb, mushrooms, leeks, or other meats and vegetables.

Popular main courses are *mitite* (grilled beef) and *tocana* (pork stew with garlic and onions). *Mamaliga*, a cornmeal dish, is often eaten with stuffed cabbage, vine leaves, or poached eggs. Rice and minced meat are wrapped in vine or cabbage leaves to make *sarmale*. Vegetables such as eggplant, peppers, or pickles often accompany the main course.

## MAMALIGA

This classic Romanian cornmeal dish is very similar to Italian polenta. *Mamaliga* can be served alone with sour cream or as a side dish with meat, fish, or eggs. Romanian recipes often call for *telemea*, a soft, creamy cheese with a tang. High-quality cottage cheese makes a good substitute.

3 cups milk

2 teaspoons salt

1 teaspoon plus 1½ tablespoons butter

1½ cups yellow cornmeal, medium or coarse ground*

6 ounces cottage cheese

1. In a heavy medium saucepan, heat the milk, salt, and one teaspoon of the butter over medium heat. Bring to a simmer.

2. Stir about one tablespoon of the cornmeal into the simmering milk mixture. When milk begins to simmer again, pour in the remaining cornmeal all at once. Immediately stir vigorously with a wooden spoon for about 1 minute. Stir in the cheese and the rest of the butter. Turn the heat down to low and continue stirring for another 10 to 15 minutes. Mamaliga will thicken and pull away from the sides of the pan.

3. Shake the pan to loosen the mamaliga. Then immediately turn the pan upside-down onto a warm serving plate. Cut the mamaliga into slices and serve hot.

Serves 4 to 6

* **The yellow cornmeal commonly found in supermarkets is medium ground. Coarse ground cornmeal (polenta) is available at Italian markets, natural food stores, and some supermarkets. Coarse polenta may require about 25 to 30 minutes cooking time.**

Romanian desserts include ice cream, cakes, pastries, pies known as *placinte,* and *baclava*—a thin pastry filled with nuts and covered with honey syrup. *Papanasi* are doughnuts made with cream and cheese. Adults also enjoy a wide variety of excellent wines, most of which are produced in Moldavia and along the Black Sea coast.

## ▶ Recreation and Sports

The Carpathian Mountains and the Black Sea coast are the busiest recreation spots in Romania. Rock climbing, hiking, snow skiing, and snowboarding are popular in the Carpathians. Vacation resorts along the Black Sea offer swimming, sailing, waterskiing, and other warm-weather sports.

The **Poiana Brasov resort** sits at the foot of Mount Postavaru. Skiing, snowboarding, hiking, and mountain biking are popular activities at the resort. Visit www.vgsbooks.com for links to more information about Romania's culture.

The country's favorite spectator sport is football, known in the United States as soccer. The government has built football stadiums in Romania's large cities and has organized professional football leagues. Many amateur sports enthusiasts participate in cycling, football, and tennis. An eighty-thousand-seat stadium in Bucharest hosts basketball, volleyball, handball, and skating events.

Romanian Olympic athletes have brought home medals in gymnastics, wrestling, and weight lifting. Romanian gymnasts, in particular, have earned international fame. Nadia Comaneci was the first athlete in history to earn perfect scores of 10 for gymnastic routines

**Gymnast Andreea Raducan** performs her floor routine at the 2000 Summer Olympic Games in Sydney, Australia. Raducan won the gold medal in the women's all-around final. But after she tested positive for pseudophedrine, a medical drug banned by the Olympic Committee, Raducan lost her gold medal to teammate Simona Amaner.

she performed in the 1976 Summer Olympic Games in Montreal, Canada. Coach Bela Karolyi led the Romanian women's gymnastics team to two Olympic wins in 1976 and 1980. In 1981 Karolyi and his wife, Marta, defected from (or left) Communist Romania for the United States. Karolyi then coached four successful U.S. women's teams in the 1984, 1988, 1992, and 1996 Olympics. Contemporary Romanian gymnastic stars include Lavinia Milosovici, Gina Gogean, Claudia Presecan, and Andreea Raducan.

# THE ECONOMY

After World War II, Romania's Communist government nationalized industries, mines, banks, transportation companies, and most retail stores. It also collectivized private farms. Government planners decided how these new nationalized and collectivized businesses were run and how much Romanian workers were paid. Under Communism, government-run business and industry is supposed to ensure equality among workers. But the Romanian government did not have the money to invest in new equipment, technology, and procedures. Over time, the country's agricultural and industrial bases became outdated, and production slowed.

Through the 1970s, Romania's population grew while production of food and other consumer goods (goods made for people to buy and use) declined. The country also needed money for new housing and infrastructure projects (such as roads, power lines, sewers, and public buildings). Romania began borrowing heavily from foreign governments. In the 1980s, Ceausescu grew determined to pay off all Romania's foreign debt. He believed the debt gave organizations such as the International

Monetary Fund (IMF) and the World Bank too much power over Romania's political affairs. To pay the debt, Romania began exporting most of the country's manufactured products and food and imported very little. This policy resulted in severe shortages for the Romanian people.

Under these pressures, Romanians became used to working around the system. They dealt on the black market—an unofficial way of buying and selling goods. They paid bribes to local officials to secure goods and services, from food to drivers' licenses. Corruption in local government and the court system became widespread.

After the fall of the Communist government in 1989, Romania's new leaders began economic reforms. They tried to create a more open market for goods and services. The government also began privatizing—selling state-owned businesses to private investors. But the outdated equipment and production methods and corruption left over from the Communist era slowed reforms. High unemployment and shortages of food and other goods continued through the 1990s.

By the early twenty-first century, Romania's economy had stabilized and began to grow. Industrial and infrastructure updates attracted foreign investors. And the IMF began lending Romania money for more projects, including construction of roads, sewer systems, and homes. Resolving the country's infrastructure problems and its corruption issues are essential to Romania's bid to join the EU in 2007. Romania hopes the EU will offer support on economic, social, and national security issues.

## ⊙ Industry, Mining, and Energy

Romania's Communist government focused on industrial and manufacturing development in the 1950s and 1960s. The Communist leadership invested heavily in industries that made durable goods, such as machinery and steel. Large government-owned firms built new plants throughout the country. In the post-Communist era, some of those firms were reorganized or broken up into smaller companies. Some plants closed, and a few companies were privatized. The reorganization of Romania's industrial core, along with aging and outdated factories, led to a decline in this sector (part) of the economy. But industry is still important. In the early 2000s, industry accounted for 34 percent of Romania's gross domestic product (GDP), the value of goods and services produced in one year.

Romanian plants produce tires, passenger cars, tractors, and airplanes. Factories in Bucharest and Galati, a city on the lower Danube, make cement and steel for the construction industry. The manufacture of aluminum, copper, and other finished metals is also important in construction and for export. Refineries convert crude oil and other petroleum products into rubber and chemicals. Other plants make electrical equipment such as radios and televisions, electronics such as computers, textiles, shoes, and finished clothing.

Energy is also an important part of Romania's industrial sector. It accounts for 5 percent of the country's industrial output and employs 6 percent of the workforce. Crude oil and natural gas are produced from offshore wells in the Black Sea. Coal mining plays a role in Romania's energy market, as it is used in thermal (steam heat) power plants. But coal production has declined since the early 1990s. Other sources of electricity include hydroelectric and nuclear power plants, wind farms, and solar energy systems. Domestic demand for electricity has increased since 2000.

## ⊙ Agriculture

Between 1948 and 1962, the Romanian government took over most of the country's private farms. It forced rural workers to join state-owned collective farms. Each collective had a planning committee, which set schedules and production goals. Farmers shared their labor and income. By the 1960s, the Romanian government owned 90 percent of the country's productive land.

Collectivization, however, did not improve harvests. Because the government invested mostly in heavy industries, little money was available for farm improvements. In addition, the government moved workers from the countryside to the cities, leaving rural areas with a shortage of farm laborers.

In the early 1990s, the government began returning farmland to private ownership. By the early 2000s, 85 percent of the nation's farmland and 98 percent of the livestock were privately owned. Farmers have taken advantage of a free market for their goods, and production of meat and grain has slowly increased. But outdated farming methods and equipment continue to limit crop yields. Also, limits on how much land a person or family can own makes each farm small and less productive. The agricultural sector employs 38 percent of the total population and 68 percent of the rural population. But it accounts for only 13 percent of the GDP.

Romania's principal crops are grains—including wheat, rye, and corn. These are mostly grown on the plains of Wallachia, Moldavia, and Banat. Farmers also grow potatoes and cabbage. They raise sunflowers for their seeds and oil and grow beets to be refined into sugar. Wine grapes thrive in Moldavia and near the Black Sea coast. Mountainous regions of Romania support fruit orchards and vineyards. Livestock raised in Romania include cattle, pigs, sheep, goats, horses, and poultry. Romania's fishing industry is strong, but it has

**Shepherds** tend their flock in Bukovina. Farmers in Romania raise more sheep than any other kind of livestock.

been affected by continuing water pollution. Carp, mackerel, and sardines are important products.

## ⊘ Transportation

During the Communist era, Romanian industry was focused on producing heavy equipment and materials such as steel and concrete. Most of these heavy industrial products were transported by railroad. Romania's government ran an extensive network of freight and passenger trains (as few people owned cars in that era). But light industry (the manufacture or assembly of products such as electronics) became more important to the economy, and transportation shifted away from railroads. Products such as electronics, textiles, and farm produce could be more easily transported in trucks. In the post-Communist era, more people owned cars too. Romania's 48,500-mile (78,000 km) road network became the primary transportation system.

The rapid growth of car and truck traffic strained the aging and poorly developed road system. Highways, streets, and bridges needed repairs. And the country needed some way to control traffic jams, accidents, and increased air pollution from car exhaust. In the 1990s, the government ministry (department) overseeing transportation was reorganized. The World Bank and some European institutions loaned Romania substantial money to update and expand its road system. The government also set up an auto registration department and truck inspection stations to check vehicles for safety and air pollution standards. Planned improvements were slowed at first by a lack of trained engineers to assess and plan road works. But upgrading roads and enforcing safety measures have brought Romania's road system closer to EU standards.

Some road traffic congestion is eased by public transportation. Bucharest has an underground train system called the metro. Other large cities have extensive bus, tram, and trolley systems.

## ROMANIAN AVIATION

Romanians have pioneered many developments in the field of aviation. In the early twentieth century, inventors such as Aurel Vlaicu and Traian Vuia developed flying machines and early airplanes. In 1910 Romanian scientist Henri Coanda built the world's first jet engine. Meanwhile, George Valentin Bibescu established Romania's first flight schools for training pilots. Transylvanian Hermann Oberth was a physicist and a pioneer in rocketry and astronautics—the fields that led to modern space exploration.

**Trams** provide transportation to beachgoers in Mamaia, a popular resort town on the Black Sea coast.

River traffic remains important to Romania's foreign trade. Commercial barges use the Danube River, the busiest waterway of central and eastern Europe. A canal connects the river with Constanta, Romania's principal port on the Black Sea. Passenger ferries also link Black Sea ports with cities along the Danube River.

For air transport, the government still owns the national airline, TAROM (Transporturile Aeriene Romane). Romania has nineteen commercial airports. Bucharest, Cluj-Napoca, and Timisoara airports serve international flights to other European cities, North America, and Asia. Other airports are used for domestic travel.

Constanta, on the Black Sea, is Romania's largest port. It handles 115 million tons (104 metric tons) of cargo each year.

## Trade

For many years, Romania's most important trading partner was the Soviet Union. This partnership linked Romania's economy with those of other Warsaw Pact countries. But in the 1960s, Romania also formed trading ties with many non-Communist countries, particularly Germany. The former Warsaw Pact countries and Germany are still Romania's biggest trading partners. Romania also trades with Italy, China, Iran, and Eastern Europe.

Fuels and raw materials make up the largest portion of Romania's foreign trade. Machinery, chemicals, furniture, textiles, aluminum, and steel products are important exports. To meet its energy needs, Romania imports coal, natural gas, and crude oil. Romanian companies also buy sugar, meat, iron ore, and cotton from abroad.

## Tourism and Service Industries

Tourism and service industries (businesses that provide services rather than goods) account for 53 percent of Romania's GDP. Since the fall of Communist governments in Eastern Europe, tourism has become an important source of income. Newly opened borders allow an increasing number of Western European tourists to visit the region. Since the early 1990s, Romania has attracted several million tourists each year. Money from tourism totals in the hundred millions yearly.

Throughout the 1990s, tourism has benefited from a favorable exchange rate. This means that Romanian prices for food, accommodations, and activities are relatively cheap for travelers from Western Europe and other part of the world. Romanian hotels have been upgraded for comfort and tourist services. Local governments have built new parks, cleaned up streets and beaches, and stepped up crime prevention. And new restaurants and cafés have opened on the streets of Bucharest and other popular cities.

There are many attractions and activities throughout Romania. Villages in Transylvania and in the northern Carpathians provide glimpses into a traditional rural way of life. Romania's magnificent castles, including the imposing Bran Castle near Brasov, attest to the

**Bran Castle,** more familiarly known as Dracula's Castle, was not actually built by Vlad III. Instead, the castle was built in 1382 by Saxons hoping to defend the area against invading Turks.

**Vlad Tepes**

## DRACULA

Vlad III (1431–1476) was a Wallachian nobleman. Vlad took the last name Dracula, meaning "the son of the dragon." He was also called Vlad Tepes, or Vlad the Impaler, for his method of killing enemies. In battle he impaled, or pierced, enemies on long stakes and left them to bleed to death. This cruel habit earned him a place in literary history. After hearing Romanian folk stories about Vlad, Irish writer Bram Stoker used him as a model for the title character in *Dracula*, a novel published in 1897. Stoker made Dracula into a supernatural monster, a vampire who drained the blood from his helpless victims. Bran Castle became associated with the Dracula legend and remains a popular tourist spot for fans of vampire books and movies.

country's long history. And the monasteries of Moldavia draw religious pilgrims and art lovers who admire the centuries-old frescoes that adorn the monasteries' walls.

Old neighborhoods—with historic architecture, churches, cafés, and bookstores—in Brasov, Sibiu, and Cluj-Napoca survived Romania's industrialization. Bucharest offers visitors fine museums and music festivals. The Village Museum in the capital preserves examples of traditional homes from around the country. Tourists who favor recreational activities visit the Carpathian Mountains for hiking and the Black Sea coast for sailing, swimming, and water-skiing.

Banking and information are growing sectors in Romania's service economy. In the late 1990s, Romania began privatizing government-owned banks. The government also began improving banking practices, such as monitoring how banks loaned and invested money. In information services, modernization of Romania's telecommunication systems began in the 1990s. The government invested in new equipment such as fiber optic cables for the country's telephone network. It also began privatizing telephone companies. The number of Romanians who own televisions and personal computers and who have access to the Internet is not as high as in other European countries. But Romania continues to grow in these areas.

## The Future

Since the end of Communism, Romanians have worked to improve their economy. But Romania's parliament has had difficulty putting new economic policies in place. And without major improvement, Romanians will continue to suffer from low wages, shortages of consumer goods, and a poor standard of living.

But Romania has a young and well-educated workforce. In some areas, this has led to dynamic growth. Romania has one of the fast-growing media markets in southeastern Europe. Before 1989 media outlets were few and were state-owned. Journalists and entertainers were subject to government control. After 1989 the number of television networks, radio stations, newspapers, and cable TV channels shot up. Bucharest has more than thirty media outlets—daily newspapers, television stations, and radio stations featuring international, national, and local news. Other large cities have their own media outlets. Media provides a wide variety of jobs, as well as reinforcing the country's connection to the rest of Europe and the world.

Romania has also become a good prospect for outsourcing. In this business strategy, companies parcel out jobs to other companies. Often the secondary companies are in countries where wages are low and workers are plentiful. Western Europe and the United States often outsource work to companies in China and India. In the early twenty-first century, Western European

## ROMANIA AND THE EU

Romania is committed to joining the EU in 2007. The EU will provide Romania with economic opportunities and support for government programs. But some EU officials are not convinced Romania is ready to join. Some are simply against expanding the EU too fast to include Eastern European countries with lingering economic and political problems. EU officials have warned the Romanian government that it is not working hard enough on reforming political corruption and human rights issues. Some European leaders have also questioned Romania's support for the United States in the Iraq war. Powerful EU leaders such as France and Germany disagreed with the U.S. decision to invade Iraq in March 2003. But Adrian Nastase has said that the Romanian government wishes to have strong relationships with both Europe and the United States.

countries began outsourcing data processing, software development, clothes manufacturing, and light industry to Eastern Europe. This trend has helped Romania's economy.

To become a successful outsourcing partner, Romania must resolve its problems with corruption, such as bribery. Such illegal practices—once routine in Communist Romania—are unacceptable to many foreign investors. Romania has also not been in a competitive free market for long, and customer service and quality issues remain. But many Romanian workers have the advantages of education, good computer skills, and multilingualism (speaking one or more foreign languages). Romanians look to a reformed government and to themselves for a successful economic future.

 Visit www.vgsbooks.com for links to discover more about Romania's economy. Convert U.S. dollars into Romanian lei, learn more about Romania's tourism industry, and more.

**2000s B.C.** The Bronze Age begins in Romania. A farming culture is created in the Danube River valley when nomads migrate from the north and west and intermix with tribes already living there.

**CA. 1000 B.C.** Dacians begin occupying the area of modern Romania.

**A.D. 101-106** The Roman army conquers Dacia. Dacia becomes a province of Rome. Roman colonists introduce Latin to the Dacians.

**271** Dacian rebels and their allies force the Roman army to withdraw.

**800s** The Magyars conquer lands along the Danube and build cities there. They eventually push south into Transylvania.

**1396** The Ottoman Empire conquers the principalities of Wallachia and Moldavia.

**1504** Stephen III is defeated and killed in a rebellion against the Turks. Moldavian princes become vassals of the Turkish sultan.

**1600** Michael the Brave brings Wallachia, Moldavia, and Transylvania under the rule of a single Romanian for the first time.

**1688** The Turks retreat from Transylvania, leaving it under rule of the Habsburg Empire.

**1791-1812** Russia and Turkey fight for Romanian territory.

**1812** The Peace of Bucharest treaty formally gives Wallachia and part of Moldavia to Turkey, and the eastern part of Moldavia to Russia.

**1830s** Romanians draw up the Organic Statutes, calling for government reform and the unification of Wallachia and Moldavia.

**1848** The Transylvanian legislature abolishes serfdom and cuts back the privileges of wealthy landowners. Austria takes control of Transylvania after helping Romanians prevent unification of the region with Hungary.

**1860s** Romanian writers start using the Roman alphabet instead of the Cyrillic, symbolizing a stronger connection to western Europe.

**1861** Moldavia and Wallachia unite to form an independent Romania.

**1862** Bucharest, the capital of Wallachia, becomes the capital of united Romania.

**1864** The the country's first higher education institution, the University of Bucharest, is founded.

**1866** Romanians hold a popular election for the first time to elect a new ruler.

**1867** Habsburg emperor Franz Joseph agrees to a dual monarchy, Austria-Hungary, allowing Hungary to take over Transylvania.

**1878** Russia and Turkey officially recognize Romanian independence and grant Romania the northern part of Dobruja.

**1881** Romania becomes a kingdom. King Carol I strengthens ties with western Europe.

**1916** Romania joins the Allies in World War I but withdraws when Central power forces defeat its army.

**1918** World War I ends. Romania takes control of Transylvania, part of the Banat region, and Bessarabia.

**1923** A new Romanian constitution is adopted, featuring land reform and modernization of industries.

**1930s** The Great Depression causes high unemployment in Romania. King Carol II assumes a dictatorship to stop unrest among political parties.

**1940** Iron Guard leader Ion Antonescu takes control of the government, and Romania joins the Axis, opposing the Allies, in World War II.

**1944** Soviets invade Romania, and King Michael overthrows Antonescu. Michael signs a peace treaty with the Soviet Union.

**1947** The Romanian Communist Party takes over the government. Industrialization improves Romania's economy.

**1955** Romania joins other Eastern European countries in signing the Warsaw Pact.

**1965** Nicolae Ceausescu comes to power in Romania. He loosens ties to the Soviet Union and forms new relationships with Western countries.

**1989** Romanians overthrow the government in December, arresting and executing Ceausescu and his wife, Elena.

**1990** Romania holds its first democratic election in forty-four years. Voters choose Ion Iliescu as the new president.

**1991** A constitution is created, guaranteeing civil rights and establishing a parliament. The new government works toward creating a free market.

**1996** Emil Constantinescu is elected president by those favoring more radical reform.

**2003** Voters approve major amendments to the constitution so that Romanian law complies with the standards of the European Union.

**2004** Traian Basescu is elected president, promising to relieve poverty and work toward EU membership. He appoints Calin Tariceanu prime minister.

**2005** A law banning foreign adoptions of Romanian children takes effect.

**2006** The Danube River overflows its banks in southwestern Romania, forcing fourteen thousand residents to flee their homes.

**Fast Facts**

COUNTRY NAME Romania

AREA 91,700 square miles (237,500 sq. km)

MAIN LANDFORMS Eastern Carpathian Mountains, Danube Delta, Transylvanian Alps, Transylvanian Plateau, Wallachian Plain, Western Carpathians

HIGHEST POINT Mount Moldoveanu, 8,343 feet (2,543 m) above sea level

LOWEST POINT Sea level

MAJOR RIVERS Arges, Danube, Dambovita, Ialomita, Mures, Olt, Siret, Somes

ANIMALS Chamois, cormorants, deer, eagles, egrets, foxes, geese, lynx, pelicans, salmon, sturgeon, trout, wild boar, wolves

CAPITAL CITY Bucharest

OTHER MAJOR CITIES Constanta, Cluj-Napoca, Brasov, Iasi, Galati, Timisoara

OFFICIAL LANGUAGE Romanian

MONETARY UNIT Leu. 100 bani = 1 leu.

**Currency**

## ROMANIAN CURRENCY

The leu (plural, lei) is the basic unit of Romanian currency. The leu's code in international banking is RON. Leu banknotes (paper money) come in 1 leu, 5 lei, 10 lei, 50 lei, 100 lei, and 500 lei. Each denomination has its own color and texture. Each also features a portrait of a famous Romanian and a symbol for that person. For example, the 5 lei note features a musical key in honor of composer Georges Enesco. A leu is subdivided into 100 bani (singular, ban). Coins come in denominations of 1 ban, 5 bani, 10 bani, and 50 bani.

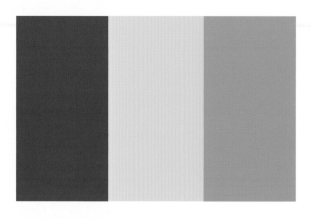

The current version of the Romanian flag was officially adopted in 1989. It has three vertical bands of equal width, in blue, yellow, and red. The use of these three colors dates back to the sixth century. They originally represented Moldavia and two parts of Wallachia. The flag for the Kingdom of Romania (1881–1947) featured a coat of arms in the center stripe. Communist Romania's flag (1947–1989) also bore a coat of arms with Communist symbols. During the 1989 revolution, protesters cut out the Communist coat of arms, leaving holes in the middle of their flags. After the revolution, the new government decided to leave the center stripe empty.

Since 1989 Romania's national anthem has been "Desteapta-te, Romane!" (Awaken Thee, Romanian!). The lyrics were written by poet Andrei Muresan. The music was composed by Anton Pann. It was originally published as "Un Rasunet" (An Echo) and sung during the 1848 revolution. In 1947 Romania's Communist government banned the song. But during the 1989 revolution, people began singing it in the streets in defiance of the Communists. Here is the English translation of two verses:

> Wake up, O Romanian, from your deathly sleep
> Into which you've been sunk by the barbaric tyrants.
> Now, as at no other time, create yourself a new fate,
> For all others to accept, even your cruelest enemies.
>
> Now, as at no other time, let's send proof to the world
> That the blood of a Romanian still flows inside these hands.
> That in our chests we still maintain our pride in a name,
> The victor in his battles, the name of Trajan!

For a link where you can listen to Romania's national anthem, "Desteapta-te Romane!" (Awaken Thee, Romanian!), visit www.vgsbooks.com

**CONSTANTIN BRANCUSI** (1876–1957) Brancusi is one of Romania's most famous and most admired modern artists. He was born in the Wallachian town of Hobita. He studied art and, in particular, sculpture in Bucharest through his early twenties. In 1904 Brancusi moved to Paris, where he was influenced by African and Asian art. He was also drawn to the abstract art movement. The movement rejected realistic depictions of human and natural forms. Abstract art instead uses simple shapes and colors to create subjective (personal or emotional) forms. Brancusi disliked the term *abstract art*, but his smooth, simple sculptures reflect the movement's influences. Brancusi sculptures, such as *Danaide, Il Bacio,* and *Bird in Space,* are exhibited in major museums throughout the world.

**ION LUCA CARAGIALE** (1852–1912) Caragiale was a playwright, novelist, and short-story writer. He was a leader of Junimea, the literary society credited with forming the basis of modern Romanian culture. Caragiale's plays often took an ironic look at Romanian society.

**NICOLAE CEAUSESCU** (1918–1989) Ceausescu was Romania's Communist leader from 1965 to 1989. After the Communist Party took over the government, Ceausescu held several prominent positions. In 1974 he was elected president. His calls for Romanian independence from the Soviet Union were at first popular. But he soon enforced a strict regime that used secret police to control the media and silence political opponents. His policies also crippled Romania's economy, causing severe food and energy shortages. During the 1989 revolution, Ceausescu's army defected to the anti-Communist demonstrators. The army captured and imprisoned Ceausescu and his wife, Elena. After a brief trial, the Ceausescus were executed by a military firing squad.

**NADIA COMANECI** (b. 1961) Comaneci has been called one of the greatest gymnasts of all time. Born in Onesti, she began practicing gymnastics at the age of six. She came to the attention of the world at the age of fourteen, in the 1976 Summer Olympics. She won three gold medals, a silver medal, and a bronze medal. She also became the first Olympic gymnast ever to score a perfect 10. She continued to compete for and teach in Romania. But in 1989, she defected to the United States, just one month before the country's anti-Communist revolution. Comaneci and her husband, U.S. Olympic gymnast Bart Conner, own a gymnastics academy in Oklahoma.

**MIHAI EMINESCU** (1850–1889) Born in Moldavia, Eminescu is considered one of Romania's greatest poets. His poems range in topics from love and nature to history and social commentary. Famous works include *Doina, Evening on the Hill, I Have Yet One Desire,* and *The Morning Star.* Eminescu also taught school and worked as a newspaper writer and editor.

**GEORGES ENESCO** (1881–1955) Enesco is one of the twentieth century's most outstanding classical musicians. Born in the village of Liveni, Enesco began studying music at the age of seven. He mastered the violin and the piano. He also became a noted composer, basing much of his work on Romanian folk music. His work includes an opera and many pieces of orchestral music (for large groups of musicians) and chamber music (for small groups). He later became an orchestra conductor and a violin teacher. The famous violinist Yehudi Menuhin was one of Enesco's students.

**ANGELA GHEORGHIU** (b. 1965) Romania's most famous modern opera singers, Gheorghiu was born in Adjud and first trained at the Bucharest Academy of Music. Gheorghiu is a soprano, a female singer of the highest vocal range. She is best known for her roles in the operas of Italian composers Giuseppe Verdi and Giacomo Puccini. Gheorghiu also performs and records Romanian opera, popular songs, and Orthodox church music.

**NICOLAE GRIGORESCU** (1838–1907) Grigorescu began his career as a painter creating religious icons for churches and monasteries. In 1861, at the age of twenty-three, Grigorescu moved to Paris to study art. He was greatly influenced by the French painters of the Barbizon school. These artists painted realistic depictions of everyday life, such as peasants doing farmwork. Grigorescu returned to Romania about 1890 and continued to paint rural subjects and landscapes. He is considered one of the founders of modern Romanian painting.

**EUGENE IONESCO** (1909–1994) Ionesco is best known as a playwright in the Theatre of the Absurd. Plays belonging to the Theatre of the Absurd often emphasize that life has no real meaning. The characters have no real identities, and the dialogue is often nonsensical or dreamlike. Ionesco's works include *The Lesson, The Chairs, Rhinoceros,* and *Exit the King.*

**ILIE NASTASE** (b. 1946) Bucharest native Nastase was one of the top professional tennis players of the 1970s and Romania's first player of international fame. Nastase won championships at the U.S. Open, the French Open, and Wimbledon (Great Britain). Nastase was considered an excellent athlete, but he was also known for his strong personality on the tennis court. Crowds often found him amusing and entertaining. But his displays of bad temper earned him the nickname Nasty. Nastase was inducted into the International Tennis Hall of Fame in 1991. In 1996 he unsuccessfully ran for mayor of Bucharest.

**BRAN CASTLE** Located on a mountain pass in southeastern Transylvania, the town of Bran was an important defensive post for many centuries. One of the castles used to guard the pass, Bran Castle, was built in the late fourteenth century. Bran Castle has become associated with a well-known figure from literature and horror movies—the vampire Count Dracula. That connection is a mistake. Dracula's real-life counterpart, Vlad III, did not build or live at Bran Castle. But the legend endures, and thousands of visitors every year line up to tour the castle and enjoy Dracula-related souvenirs.

**BUKOVINA'S PAINTED MONASTERIES** The Bukovina region of Moldavia is the site of Romania's famous painted monasteries and churches. In the sixteenth century, fresco artists painted the religious buildings inside and out with scenes from biblical stories and historical events. The frescoes told visual stories to peasants who could not read. Some of the frescoes have been damaged by age and the weather, but many others have been preserved and restored. Some of the best examples are in Humor, Moldovita, Sucevita, and Voronet.

**COTROCENI PALACE** This historic building lies along the banks of the Dambovita River in Bucharest. King Ferdinand I had the palace built in the 1890s for his wife, Marie. It served as a royal residence until 1947. The palace currently serves as the residence of the Romanian president. It also houses the Cotroceni National Museum, dedicated to local history and culture. The palace is part of a complex called the Cotroceni Ensemble. The ensemble originally included a seventeenth-century monastery and church, but the church was destroyed by the Ceausescu government in 1985.

**DACIAN FORTRESSES** Archaeologists consider southwest Transylvania the cradle of Dacian civilization. Traces of Dacian life, such as pottery, weapons, and the ruins of mines and buildings, are found throughout the region. In the Orastie Mountains south of the modern city of Hunedoara lie the ruins of several Dacian citadels (fortresses used to guard an area). The citadels date from the first century B.C. and the first century A.D. Dacians built the fortresses to guard their capital, Sarmizegetusa.

**DANUBE DELTA** The Danube Delta in the Dobruja region was greatly damaged by human pollution throughout most of the twentieth century. Animal and plant life were damaged by sewage and industrial waste. The area's reeds, which naturally filter the water and provide habitats, were carelessly harvested. But since the 1990s, large parts of the delta have been strictly protected as nature reserves. Tourists can take eco-friendly (not damaging to the environment) trips to see the delta's wide variety of plants and trees, birds, fish, and small mammals.

**MARAMURES'S WOODEN CHURCHES** The county of Maramures in Transylvania is home to Orthodox churches important for their architecture and history. Maramures was an isolated place, and the people there developed a strong sense of community. Much of community life centered on the local church. During the eighteenth century, local builders and artisans (people trained and skilled in making certain items) took great care in crafting and decorating small wooden churches. They took particular pride in building tall clock towers on each church. Eight of these wooden churches remain in Maramures.

**SIGHISOARA** This Transylvanian city of 32,000 was first a Dacian settlement, then a Roman town, then an important urban center filled with merchants and crafters. It is famous for its historic buildings, many of which date to the Middle Ages. The Citadel was built in the twelfth century as a fortress. Along its 0.5 mile (1 km) defensive wall are nine towers built by medieval workers, including the Tinsmiths' Tower, the Tailors' Tower, and the Shoemakers' Tower. The fourteenth-century Clock Tower still rises above the skyline. The clock's mechanism includes carved wooden soldiers, goddesses, and other figures, which emerge from slots to show the days of the week. The city is also home to the Church on the Hill, the Monastery Church, and a 175-step covered staircase. Along with historic sites, Sighisoara has many winding streets filled with centuries-old homes and cafes. Each summer the city hosts a Medieval Festival, with costumed street performers, music, and plays.

**collectivism:** a political theory that argues for collecting businesses under one group's control, rather than allowing individual ownership. In Communist countries, farms were often collectivized. Farmers had to give up control of their own properties and join a collective, which was controlled by the government.

**Communist:** of or belonging to the Communist Party. The Communist Party follows the political philosophy of Communism. Communism argues that equality among people is only truly possible if workers control the economy. Workers control the economy by controlling the production and distribution of all goods from farms and factories. In most Communist countries, a one-party Communist government controls production and distribution on behalf of the workers.

**corruption:** the illegal practices of a government or governmental agency, such as a police force or a court system. Corruption often includes officials taking bribes for special treatment and stealing money from government funds.

**Dacians:** the early inhabitants of the region that became Romania. Known first to the Greeks as the Getae, the Dacians lived mostly in Transylvania. Historians estimate that at the height of their civilization, Dacians numbered about 2 million. They were mainly farmers, growing cereals (such as wheat) and fruits and raising sheep and cattle. They also traded food, cloth, salt, lumber, and other products with neighboring tribes and with the Greeks and Romans. The Dacians were accomplished metalworkers. They created gold and silver jewelry and forged iron and bronze weapons.

**delta:** a wedge of land that forms at the mouth of a river where it flows into a sea or another larger body of water. Deltas are formed by sediment—sand, soil, clay, and small stones—carried by the river. When the outgoing flow of the river is slowed by the coastal currents of the sea, the sediment builds up to form a delta.

**Eastern Orthodox Christianity:** referring to religious beliefs and rites practiced in Eastern Europe and Greece. Eastern Orthodox Christianity came about after the Great Schism of 1054. The schism, or break, developed between the hierarchy (ruling body of priests) of western and eastern European Christianity over religious doctrine and leadership. The western church became the Roman Catholic Church, and the eastern church became the Eastern Orthodox Church.

**European Union (EU):** an organization of European countries that promotes cooperation among its members in matters of politics and economics

**free market:** a type of economy in which goods and services are freely sold in a competitive situation

**gross domestic product (GDP):** a measure of the total value of goods and services produced within a country in a certain amount of time (usually one year). A similar measure is gross national product (GNP). GDP and GNP are often measured in terms of purchasing power parity (PPP). PPP converts values to international dollars, making it possible to compare how much similar goods and services cost to the residents of different countries.

*Glossary*

**hydroelectric:** electric power generated by moving or falling water. Hydroelectric power plants usually use dams, or barriers, to control the flow of water. Water released from a dam drives turbines (rotating engines), which generate the electricity.

**infrastructure:** the system of public works, such as sewers, paved roads, bridges, and electrical plants, built to support a community

**nationalism:** a political ideology that strongly emphasizes a nation's culture and interests as more important than those of other nations

**parliamentary:** referring to a system of government formed by a prime minister and a parliament (a body of elected officials). The prime minister is the head of government. In Romania the prime minister is nominated by the president, and the nomination must be confirmed by the parliament. The parliament is made up of legislators (lawmakers) from the prime minister's party and from other parties. The prime minister and the parliament must work together to pass laws and rule the country. If they cannot successfully work together over time, the parliament may vote to remove the prime minister. The prime minister may also dissolve the parliament and call for new elections.

**privatization:** a process that changes businesses and industry from government control to private ownership. Privatization is often used to try to reduce government costs and improve service by allowing for market competition.

**unification:** the act or process of a number of smaller governments coming together to form a political union. Romania's unification began in 1861 with the union of Moldavia and Wallachia. Throughout the nineteenth and early twentieth centuries, unification grew to include Transylvania, Dobruja, and the other regions that make up modern Romania.

**BBC News. 2006.**
http://news.bbc.co.uk **(March 8, 2006).**
The World Edition of the BBC (British Broadcasting System) news is updated throughout the day, every day. It contains political and cultural news, as well as country profiles, including Romania.

**Boia, Lucian. *Romania*. London: Reaktion Books, 2004.**
University of Bucharest professor Boia examines Romania's history, culture, and people, including the country's current problems and international relations.

**Central Intelligence Agency (CIA). 2006.**
http://www.cia.gov/cia/publications/factbook/geos/ro.html **(January 4, 2006).**
The World Factbook section of the CIA's website contains basic information on Romania's geography, people, economy, government, communications, transportation, military, and other issues.

***Economist*. 2006.**
http://economist.com **(March 8, 2006).**
The *Economist's* website contains articles on the current economic, political, and social situation of Romania.

**Georgescu, Vlad. *The Romanians: A History*. Edited by Matei Calinescu. Translated by Alexandra Bley-Vroman. Columbus: Ohio State University Press, 1991. Originally published as *Istoria romanilor: De la origini pina in zilele noastre* (American Romanian Academy of Arts and Sciences, 1984).**
Georgescu's detailed history of the Romanian people includes ethnic origins, society from the Middle Ages through modern times, cultural institutions, and politics.

***International Herald Tribune*. 2006.**
http://www.iht.com/ **(March 8, 2006).**
The *International Herald Tribune's* site is a source for Romanian news, news analysis, sports, and culture.

**Kokker, Steve, and Cathyn Kemp. *Romania and Moldova*. Oakland: Lonely Planet, 2004.**
The Lonely Planet guide to Romania features brief but extensive listings of sights to see and things to do. The guide also offers political, historical, and cultural notes, and up-to-date information on life in Romania.

**Population Reference Bureau. 2006.**
http://www.prb.org **(January 4, 2006).**
The annually updated statistics on this site provide demographic information for Romania and other countries. Data includes birthrates, death rates, infant mortality rates, and percentage of the population with HIV/AIDS.

***Romania: A Country Study*, 2005.**
http://memory.loc.gov/frd/cs/rotoc.html **(March 8, 2006).**
This site, produced by the Library of Congress, offers a useful research guide to Romania. The site includes information on Romania's history, geography, society, environment, culture, economy, and politics.

Selected Bibliography

**Gonczol-Davies, Ramona, and Dennis Deletant.** *Colloquial Romanian.* **London: Routledge, 2002.**
Offering a "complete course for beginners," this book and audio CD set provides easy-to-follow Romanian grammar and vocabulary lessons.

**Klepper, Nicolae.** *An Illustrated History of Romania.* **New York: Hippocrene Books, 2003.**
Klepper's concise history tells the story of the evolution of the Romanian people and the development of the modern state of Romania. Each chapter includes a section recounting simultaneous events in other parts of Europe.

**————.** *Taste of Romania.* **New York: Hippocrene Books, 1999.**
Klepper offers a taste of traditional Romanian dishes and modern innovations. The book combines more than 140 recipes with folklore, humor, art, poetry, and proverbs.

**Romanian Tourism**
http://www.romaniatourism.com
This website is hosted by the Romania National Tourist Office. It features detailed information about the country and its major cities. The Tourist Attractions section offers information on medieval towns, castles and fortresses, painted monasteries, spas and resorts, and the Danube Delta. A Special Interest section covers art and architecture, folklore, the Dracula legend, festivals and events, and other areas.

**Sharp, Anne Wallace.** *The Gypsies.* **San Diego: Lucent Books, 2002.**
Sharp examines the historical origins and migration of the Roma. She also looks at Roma family life, conflicts with authorities, social customs, and modern life. The book includes historical and modern photographs.

**Stoker, Bram.** *The Annotated Dracula.* **Edited by Leonard Wolf. New York: Crown Publishing, 1975.**
Count Dracula may be Romania's most famous fictional character. But he was created by an Irish writer who had never been to Romania. Bram Stoker wrote *Dracula* in 1897 after researching Romanian and eastern European folklore and vampire tales. This reprint of the classic novel includes maps, illustrations, and extensive comments by noted Dracula scholar Wolf.

*United Nations Educational, Scientific, and Cultural Organization (UNESCO)*
http://whc.unesco.org/
UNESCO's World Heritage Centre's website contains basic information on Romania's several World Heritage sites. UNESCO has listed these places and buildings as having outstanding natural and cultural importance.

*vgsbooks.com*
http://www.vgsbooks.com
Visit vgsbooks.com, the home page of the Visual Geography Series®. You can get linked to all sorts of useful online information, including geographical, historical, demographic, cultural, and economic websites. The vgsbooks.com site is a great resource for late-breaking news and statistics.

**Captions for photos appearing on cover and chapter openers:**

Cover: Both Roman Catholic and Orthodox cathedrals dot the skyline in Alba Iulia.

pp. 4–5 The village of Biertan in southeastern Transylvania is best known for its Saxon church set within two and a half rings of walls. This church is the best known of all Saxon churches and is listed on UNESCO's World Heritage List.

pp. 8–9 The city of Sighisoara is in the heart of Transylvania. A popular attraction there is the fourteenth-century Clock Tower (or Council Tower). This tower was once used to control the main gates of the city's defensive wall and to store ammunition, food, and the city's treasures. The clock was added to the tower in the seventeenth century.

pp. 20–21 Ruins of a Roman temple lie near ruins of a large Dacian settlement at Sarmizegetusa in Transylvania. Sarmizegetusa was Dacia's capital until the Dacians were defeated by Roman emperor Trajan's army in A.D. 106. After the victory, the Romans built a military outpost and eventually a town near the site.

pp. 36–37 Children sing at a folk festival in Maramures, a remote region in northwestern Romania. This region has remained virtually unchanged for hundreds of years, with traditional music, costumes, ancient festivals, hand-built wooden churches, and medieval farming methods still in practice.

pp. 44–45 The Curtea de Arges Monastery, and Episcopal cathedral, was built between 1514 and 1526. Legend has it that the wife of the master stonemason, Manole, was entombed in the stone walls of the church according to a local custom that required a loved one to be buried alive within the church to ensure success of the stonemason's work. The current facade of the monastery dates from 1875, when a French architect saved the building from demolition.

pp. 56–57 A power plant in Mures. Romania's industry has made improvements since the end of Communist rule in the country.

## Photo Acknowledgments

The images in this book are used with the permission of: Romanian National Tourist Office, pp. 4–5, 7, 8–9, 13, 17, 18, 19, 36–37, 39, 44–45, 48, 50, 54, 59, 62, 63; © XNR Productions, pp. 6, 11; © Marcel Baciu/Art Directors, p. 10; © age fotostock/SuperStock, pp. 14 (both), 20–21; © Dr. Peter Mercea/Art Directors, pp. 15, 40; © Hulton Archive/Getty Images, pp. 23, 27; © CORBIS, p. 29; © Martin Barlow/Art Directors, p. 33; © Pierre Andrieu/AFP/Getty Images, p. 35; © Florin Andreescu/Art Directors, p. 38; © Malcolm Fairman/Art Directors, p. 41; © Silvio Fiore/SuperStock, p. 49; © SuperStock, Inc./SuperStock, p. 51; © Reuters/CORBIS, p. 55; © Th-foto Werbung/Art Directors, pp. 56–57; © Chris Rennie/Art Directors, p. 61; © Todd Strand/Independent Picture Service, p. 68 (both); Laura Westlund, p. 69.

Cover photo: Romanian National Tourist Office. Back cover: NASA